Table of Contents

Student Table of Contents

How to Use This Guide

For Students

The Grammar Guide is designed to help you understand English grammar so that you can write and speak accurately. Each unit has been carefully structured to help you to find information easily and to develop your knowledge of English grammar.

When you are using a resource to edit written assignments and to improve your accuracy when speaking, it is essential to know how to find what you need. This reference book is constructed in a way that will help you find information on your own.

At the beginning of the guide, you will find the Table of Contents. This provides the content of each unit. Search the Table of Contents for general information. If you are not familiar with the terminology, go to the Student Table of Contents that follows it. Here, each section includes an example to help you identify the grammar rule. For instance, if you want to conjugate a regular verb such as *walk* in the simple past tense, you will find it in Unit 4 Verbs: Simple Tenses under the subsection 4.2 Simple Past Tense. In the Student Table of Contents you will find an example of the simple past tense of a regular verb, "I **played** soccer last Saturday."

At the end of *The Grammar Guide*, there is an alphabetical index of every important element of the book. Search through the Index for more specific information. For instance, if you are looking for the plural form of the noun *child*, you will look under *plural* in the Index.

The Structure of a Unit

The Grammar Guide is divided into twenty colour-coded units.
Each unit is structured in the same way.

The unit number helps you identify the unit.

The title of the unit tells you what the unit is about.

The examples at the beginning demonstrate the grammar rules that will be explained in the unit.

Most units are divided into subsections. You can easily identify them by their numbers.

The subsections of each unit have recurring questions.

Questions beginning with *What* explain the meaning of the grammar rule.

Questions beginning with *When do you use* explain the different situations where you apply the grammar rule.

Questions beginning with *How do you form* explain the formation rules so you can use the grammar rule in a sentence.

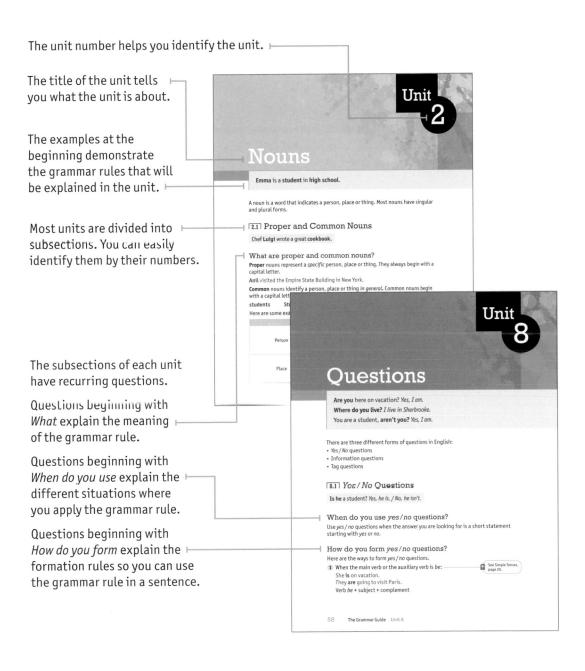

Unit 2

Nouns

Emma is a **student** in **high school**.

A noun is a word that indicates a person, place or thing. Most nouns have singular and plural forms.

2.1 Proper and Common Nouns

Chef **Luigi** wrote a great **cookbook**.

What are proper and common nouns?
Proper nouns represent a *specific* person, place or thing. They always begin with a capital letter.
Anil visited the Empire State Building in New York.
Common nouns identify a person, place or thing *in general*. Common nouns begin with a capital lett...
students   St...
Here are some exa...

| Person |
| Place |

Unit 8

Questions

Are you here on vacation? *Yes, I am.*
Where do you live? *I live in Sherbrooke.*
You are a student, **aren't you?** *Yes, I am.*

There are three different forms of questions in English:
• *Yes/No* questions
• Information questions
• Tag questions

8.1 *Yes/No* Questions

Is he a student? *Yes, he is. / No, he isn't.*

When do you use *yes/no* questions?
Use *yes/no* questions when the answer you are looking for is a short statement starting with *yes* or *no*.

How do you form *yes/no* questions?
Here are the ways to form *yes/no* questions.
1 When the main verb or the auxiliary verb is *be*:
   See Simple Tenses, page 20.
   She **is** on vacation.
   They **are** going to visit Paris.
   Verb *be* + subject + complement

58   The Grammar Guide   Unit 8

The Grammar Guide   **How to Use This Guide**   ix

Throughout the book, you will find special features:

Be Careful! shows common errors with examples of incorrect and correct usage.

▽ **BE CAREFUL!**

It's a mistake to add an *s* to the end of the nouns *information* and *homework*. They are non-count nouns.

Incorrect: I need some ~~informations~~.   Correct: I need some **information**.

Incorrect: We have a lot of ~~homeworks~~.   Correct: We have a lot of **homework**.

Cross-references help you connect one grammar rule to another.

Exceptions shows you how some words do not follow the general rules.

❋ **EXCEPTIONS**

- Some nouns have only a plural form.
  scissors   jeans   trousers   pants
  My **pants are** dirty. (plural verb) ⊣ *See Simple Present Tense, page 18.*
- Some nouns always take the singular form of the verb.
  news   series   species
  subjects such as physics *and* gymnastics
  That **species is** rare. (singular verb)
- Some nouns do not change form when they become plural.
  fish   sheep   deer
  A black **sheep** is eating.   **All the sheep** are eating.
- Some nouns can have either a regular or an irregular plural.
  cactus → cacti or cactuses   medium → media or mediums

Pronunciation shows how to pronounce problematic words.

💬 **PRONUNCIATION**

There are three ways to pronounce the final *s* in plurals.

/S/ sound for nouns ending in a *f, k, p, t* or *th* sound (unvoiced consonants)	/Z/ sound for nouns ending in a *b, d, g, l, m, n, ng, r, th, v, w* or *y* sound (voiced consonants) or any vowel sound	/IZ/ sound for nouns ending in a *dg, s, sh, tch, x* or *z* sound
beliefs, graphs	jobs	badges
packs, picnics	times	crosses
maps, tapes	songs	brushes, watches
cats, kites	bathes	boxes
breaths, months	zoos	mazes

Note that *th* is listed twice. In the first column, *th* is unvoiced: the sound comes only from your tongue and teeth. In the second column, *th* is voiced: sound comes also from your voice.

More Information provides extra information about the grammar rule.

❓ **MORE INFORMATION**

The expression *used to* is in the simple past tense because it describes a habit, routine or past situation that is no longer relevant in the present.

She **used to** eat junk food every day, but now she only eats healthy food.

Basics

I was born at three thirty a.m. on Monday, February 2, 1999.

Repeat that, please.

⌈1.1⌉ Cardinal and Ordinal Numbers

I'm going to invite **a hundred** people to my **eighteenth** birthday party.

What are cardinal numbers?

Cardinal numbers are the numbers used in simple counting.

0	zero	14	fourteen	28	twenty-eight	
1	one	15	fifteen	29	twenty-nine	
2	two	16	sixteen	30	thirty	
3	three	17	seventeen	31	thirty-one	
4	four	18	eighteen	40	forty	
5	five	19	nineteen	50	fifty	
6	six	20	twenty	60	sixty	
7	seven	21	twenty-one	70	seventy	
8	eight	22	twenty-two	80	eighty	
9	nine	23	twenty-three	90	ninety	
10	ten	24	twenty-four	100	a/one hundred	
11	eleven	25	twenty-five	1000	a/one thousand	
12	twelve	26	twenty-six	1 000 000	a/one million	
13	thirteen	→	27	twenty-seven	1 000 000 000	a/one billion

When the numbers *hundred, thousand, million* and *billion* follow a specific number, they are always written in the singular.

two hundred
three thousand
four million
ten billion

When they do not follow a specific number, they add an **s** in the plural form.

There were **thousands** of people at the parade.

What is an ordinal number?

An ordinal number refers to the position of something in a series.

Anna is the **first** student in her class to finish her exams.
Jack is celebrating his **twelfth** birthday today.

Here is a list of ordinal numbers.

1st	first	15th	fifteenth	29th	twenty-ninth
2nd	second	16th	sixteenth	30th	thirtieth
3rd	third	17th	seventeenth	31st	thirty-first
4th	fourth	18th	eighteenth	40th	fortieth
5th	fifth	19th	nineteenth	50th	fiftieth
6th	sixth	20th	twentieth	60th	sixtieth
7th	seventh	21st	twenty-first	70th	seventieth
8th	eighth	22nd	twenty-second	80th	eightieth
9th	ninth	23rd	twenty-third	90th	ninetieth
10th	tenth	24th	twenty-fourth	99th	ninety-ninth
11th	eleventh	25th	twenty-fifth	100th	a/one hundredth
12th	twelfth	26th	twenty-sixth	1000th	a/one thousandth
13th	thirteenth	27th	twenty-seventh	1 000 000th	a/one millionth
14th	fourteenth	28th	twenty-eighth	1 000 000 000th	a/one billionth

1.2 Telling Time

What time is it?

It's **two fifteen.**

It's **a quarter past two.**

How do you tell the time?

There are two ways of telling time: from a digital clock and from an analog clock.

Telling digital time

Start the sentence with ***It's*** and then read the numbers in the order they appear.

| 2:45 | It's **two forty-five.** |

| 3:20 | It's **three twenty.** |

| 5:35 | It's **five thirty-five.** |

| 21:55 | It's **nine fifty-five.** |

Telling analog time

Start the sentence with ***It's*** and then read the minutes before the hour.

 It's **a quarter** past two.　　　 It's **half** past two.

 It's **twenty** past two　　　 It's **a quarter** to two.

Remember:

1 Use the word ***past*** to indicate a time that comes after the hour but before the half hour.

 It's twenty **past** nine.

2 Use the word **_to_** to indicate a time that comes before the hour, between half past and the full hour.

 It's twenty **to** nine.

3 When referring to the exact hour, add the word **_o'clock_** after the number.

 It's eight **o'clock**.

Time markers

Use the twelve-hour clock. To differentiate between day and night when telling time, use time markers.

Time markers	Examples
a.m. (after midnight)	It's two a.m.
p.m. (past midday)	It's two p.m.
in the morning	It's two o'clock in the morning.
in the afternoon	It's two o'clock in the afternoon.
in the evening	It's eight o'clock in the evening.
at night	It's eleven o'clock at night.

 MORE INFORMATION

The abbreviations *a.m.* and *p.m.* come from Latin:

a.m. stands for *ante meridiem* (before midday).
p.m. stands for *post meridiem* (after midday).

BE CAREFUL!

When telling time, we say *at night* and not *in the night*.

Incorrect: The restaurant closes at twelve o'clock ~~in the night~~.

Correct: The restaurant closes at twelve o'clock **at night**.

1.3 Days

It's my birthday **on Monday.**

What are the days of the week?

The days of the week can be grouped into two categories.

Weekdays	Weekend days
Monday, Tuesday, Wednesday, Thursday, Friday	Saturday, Sunday

How do you refer to the days of the week?

Use the preposition **on** to refer to the days of the week.
The days of the week always start with a capital letter.

On Monday, I will go to work.
He is playing football **on Sunday.**

See Prepositions, page 94.

▽ **BE CAREFUL!**

Don't confuse *Tuesday* and *Thursday*.

Sunday	Monday	**Tuesday**	Wednesday	**Thursday**	Friday	Saturday

1.4 Months, Seasons and Dates

My birthday is **in February.**

I was born **on February 2, 1999.**

What are the months of the year?

These are the twelve months of the year:

January	February	March	April	May	June
July	August	September	October	November	December

Months always begin with a capital letter.

What are the four seasons?

These are the four seasons:

Season	Months
spring	March, April, May
summer	June, July, August
autumn / fall	September, October, November
winter	December, January, February

The four seasons are written without
a capital letter unless they are used as a proper noun. See Nouns, page 9.

In **winter**, we go skiing.
I watched the **Winter** Olympics.

How do you write the date?

You can write the date with or without the day of the week.

Saturday, June 15**,** 2013   June 15**,** 2013

In the first example, notice that there is a comma after the day of the week.
In both examples, notice that there is a comma between the day of the month
and the year.

Dates, months and seasons in a sentence

In general, use the preposition **on** to write the date in a sentence.

My birthday is **on February 2**.

Use the preposition **in** to write only the month, the season or the year.

His vacation is **in May**.
She was born **in 2001**.
We will visit France **in the summer**.
In summer, we always go to the beach.  See Prepositions, page 94.

1.5 Imperative Sentences

Turn off the light and **go** to sleep!

What is an imperative sentence?

An imperative sentence expresses instructions, warnings, suggestions or advice. The imperative sentence uses only the base form of the verb without the subject. The subject is understood.

When do you use the imperative sentence?

Use the imperative sentence for the following situations:

* To give instructions
  Open your books to page 11, please.
* To give a warning
  Wait!
* To make suggestions
  Write about your summer in California.
* To offer advice
  Don't worry.
* To offer something to someone
  Have a chocolate. **Take** two.

How do you form the verb in an imperative sentence?

Here are the ways to form the verb in an imperative sentence. Note that the verb has the same form whether the subject is singular or plural.

Affirmative form	Negative form
Verb (+ complement)	*Do not* (*Don't*) + verb (+ complement)
Write your name on the paper.	**Do not throw** your pencil at her! Please **don't speak** while I'm speaking!

Other uses

1. It is possible to use someone's name in an imperative sentence and, therefore, to state the subject. Write the name at the beginning or at the end of the sentence. Separate the name from the rest of the sentence with a comma.
   Emily, don't go too fast!   Sit down**, Joe.**
2. It is also possible to use the imperative form with the expression **let's**.
   Let's go**, Tyler.**

1.6 Basic Sentence Structure

I have a dog.

What is a sentence?

A sentence is a group of words that expresses a complete idea and that contains a subject and a verb.

How do you form a sentence?

Here is the way to form a simple sentence.

Affirmative form	Subject	+	main verb	+	complement	
	She		works		hard.	
	Tarek and Kayla		are		students.	
	Subject	+	verb *be*		main verb	+	complement
	We		are		eating		pizza.
Negative form	Subject	+	verb *do* + not	+	main verb	+	complement
	I		do not (don't)		drink		milk.
	Subject	+	verb *be* + not	+	complement	
	He		is not (isn't)		hungry.	
	Subject	+	verb *be* + not	+	main verb	+	complement
	We		are not (aren't)		eating		pizza.
Interrogative form	Verb *do*	+	subject	+	main verb	+	complement
	Do		you		have		four cats?
	Verb *be*	+	subject	+	complement	
	Is		she		your teacher?	
	Verb *be*	+	subject	+	main verb	+	complement
	Are		you		eating		pizza?

Punctuation and capitalization

A sentence always starts with a capital letter and ends with a period, an exclamation mark or a question mark.

See Punctuation, page 108.

I like pizza**. T**his pizza tastes great**! C**an I have another slice**?**

Nouns

Emma is a **student** in **high school**.

A noun is a word that indicates a person, place or thing. Most nouns have singular and plural forms.

[2.1] Proper and Common Nouns

Chef **Luigi** wrote a great **cookbook**.

What are proper and common nouns?

Proper nouns represent a *specific* person, place or thing. They always begin with a capital letter.

Anil visited the Empire State Building in New York.

Common nouns identify a person, place or thing *in general.* Common nouns begin with a capital letter only when they start a sentence or are part of a title.

students   **Students** are visiting from Ontario.

Here are some examples:

	Proper nouns	Common nouns
Person	Mark	man
	Julie	teacher
	Céline Dion	singer
Place	Canada	country
	The Eastern Townships	region
	Calgary	city

	Proper nouns	Common nouns
Thing	The Gazette	newspaper
	New Year's Day	holiday
	War and Peace	book

How do you form plural nouns?

Regular plurals

Follow these rules to form regular plurals.

Rule	Example
Most nouns: add **s**	cat → cat**s**
Nouns ending with a consonant + *y*: change *y* to *i* and add **es**	baby → bab**ies**
Nouns ending in *ch*, *s*, *sh*, *x*, *z* or *o*: add **es** But if *ch* is pronounced "k," add **s**	brush → brush**es** box → box**es** potato → potato**es** stomach → stomach**s**
Most nouns ending in *f* or *fe*: change the *f* or *fe* to **v** and add **es**	leaf → lea**ves** knife → kni**ves**
Other nouns ending in *f* or *fe*: add **s**	belief → belief**s** chef → chef**s**
Nouns with a vowel before the final *o*: add **s**	zoo → zoo**s**

Irregular plurals

An irregular plural changes part of the spelling of the singular noun. Here are the most common irregular plural nouns.

Singular form	Plural form	Singular form	Plural form
analysis	analyses	goose	geese
cactus	cacti	hypothesis	hypotheses
child	children	louse	lice
crisis	crises	man	men
criterion	criteria	medium	media
die	dice	mouse	mice
foot	feet	oasis	oases

Singular form	Plural form
ox	oxen
person	people
phenomenon	phenomena

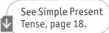

Singular form	Plural form
stimulus	stimuli
tooth	teeth
woman	women

 EXCEPTIONS

- Some nouns have only a plural form.

  scissors   jeans   trousers   pants

  My **pants are** dirty. (plural verb) ⟶ ↓ See Simple Present Tense, page 18.

- Some nouns always take the singular form of the verb.

  news   series   species

  subjects such as physics *and* gymnastics

  That **species is** rare. (singular verb)

- Some nouns do not change form when they become plural.

  fish   sheep   deer

  A black **sheep** is eating.   **All the sheep** are eating.

- Some nouns can have either a regular or an irregular plural.

  cactus → cacti or cactuses   medium → media or mediums

 PRONUNCIATION

There are three ways to pronounce the final *s* in plurals.

/S/ sound for nouns ending in a *f, k, p, t* or *th* sound (unvoiced consonants)	/Z/ sound for nouns ending in a *b, d, g, l, m, n, ng, r, th, v, w* or *y* sound (voiced consonants) or any vowel sound	/IZ/ sound for nouns ending in a *dg, s, sh, tch, x* or *z* sound
beliefs, graphs	jobs	badges
packs, picnics	times	crosses
maps, tapes	songs	brushes, watches
cats, kites	bathes	boxes
breaths, months	zoos	mazes

Note that *th* is listed twice. In the first column, *th* is unvoiced: the sound comes only from your tongue and teeth. In the second column, *th* is voiced: sound comes also from your voice.

⌐2.2⌐ Possessive Form

I took **Alex's dog** for a walk.

What is the possessive form of a noun?

The possessive form of a noun indicates that something belongs to somebody.

How do you form the possessive?

Use the apostrophe (**'**) to show possession.

1 For most singular nouns, add **'s**.

the **girl's** room   **David's** bicycle

2 For plural nouns that end in *s*, add only an apostrophe.

her **parents'** professions   the **students'** books

3 For irregular plural nouns, add **'s**.

the **children's** toys   **men's** basketball

4 For proper nouns that end in *s*, add **'s** or an apostrophe only.

Tess's book   **Tess'** book

▽ **BE CAREFUL!**

Adding **'s** or **s'** to a noun changes the meaning of the word.

the **boy's** house = the house belonging to only one boy
the **boys'** house = the house belonging to two or more boys

⌐2.3⌐ Count and Non-Count Nouns

I have five **dollars** in my wallet. (count)

I have **money** in my wallet. (non-count)

What are count and non-count nouns?

Count nouns have both a singular and a plural form. They refer to people or things that you can count.

I have to buy some **eggs.**

Non-count nouns do not have a plural form. They refer to things that you usually cannot count.

I have to buy some **coffee**.

To express quantity for non-count nouns, use measurement words such as *cup*, *glass*, *sheet* and *slice* + the preposition *of*.

This recipe asks for a **cup of** sugar.
Could I have a **glass of** water?
I need a **sheet of** paper.
Would you like a **slice of** pizza?

 BE CAREFUL!

It's a mistake to add an *s* to the end of the nouns *information* and *homework*. They are non-count nouns.

Incorrect: I need some ~~informations~~. Correct: I need some **information**.

Incorrect: We have a lot of ~~homeworks~~. Correct: We have a lot of **homework**.

Here are examples of non-count nouns.

Categories	Examples
Abstract concepts	advice, courage, fun, information
Activities or sports	homework, music, reading, soccer
Food	bread, butter, fish, meat, popcorn
Gases	air, oxygen, smog, smoke, steam
Groups of similar items	furniture, luggage, mail, money
Liquids	blood, coffee, gasoline, water
Materials	chalk, cotton, glue, wood
Natural phenomena	rain, snow, thunder, weather
Particles or grains	corn, dust, flour, rice, sugar
Subjects or fields of study	geography, drama, photography

2.4 Compound Nouns

I saw a **car accident.**

What is a compound noun?

A compound noun is formed by combining two (or more) words.

note + book = notebook

How do you form compound nouns?

Compound nouns have different forms. They can be written in the following ways:

1 As one word (without a space or hyphen):

footprint
pancake
toothbrush

2 With a space between the words:

post office
tennis racket
washing machine

3 With a hyphen between the words:

eye-opener
great-aunt
grown-up

Use a dictionary to check the correct way to write a compound noun.

Plural compound nouns

See page 10.

In a compound noun, the first word usually functions as an adjective. The second word forms the plural. Here are some examples:

Singular form	Plural form
dishwasher	dishwasher**s**
grandchild	grandchild**ren**
toothbrush	toothbrush**es**
soccer shoe	soccer shoe**s**
front-runner	front-runner**s**

Some hyphenated compound nouns form the plural by adding an **s** to the first word before the hyphen.

passer-by → passer**s**-by
brother-in-law → brother**s**-in-law

Types of compound nouns

Here are combinations used to form compound nouns.

Combinations	Compound nouns
noun + noun	homework
verb + noun	swimming pool
noun + verb	haircut
noun + adverb	passer-by
adjective + noun	greenhouse
adverb + noun	bystander

Articles

The rock star is singing on **the** stage.

A music concert is **an** exciting event.

There are three articles: *the* (definite article) and *a* or *an* (indefinite articles). Articles precede the nouns they specify. ⟶ ⬆ See Nouns, page 9.

When do you use articles?

Follow these rules for using articles.

Article	Usage	Examples
1 The **definite** article *the* refers to a *specific* person, place or thing.	• important titles	**the** Prime Minister of Canada
	• unique things or people	**the** Earth, **the** Cree
	• bodies of water (oceans, rivers, seas)	**the** Pacific Ocean **the** Fraser River
	• decades, centuries and historic periods	**The** 1960s were a great time for rock music.
	• newspapers, buildings and hotels	**The** Gazette **The** Taj Mahal **The** Plaza Hotel
	• non-count nouns that are described specifically	**The** coffee was good.
2 The **indefinite** articles *a* and *an* refer to *a general* person, place or thing.	Use *a* with singular common nouns that start with a consonant sound.	She has **a** dog.
	Use *an* with singular common nouns that start with a vowel sound (including a silent *h*).	Do you want **an** apple? The journey will take **an** hour.

→

Article	Usage	Examples
3 **No article**	Do not use an article in front of any of these:	
	• Non-specific plural nouns	• On our trip, we saw **lakes**, **mountains** and **beaches**. • The shop sells **books**, **magazines** and **newspapers**.
	• Sports	• My favourite sport is **soccer**.
	• Academic subjects	• I love **mathematics**.
	• Colours	• She thinks **red** is best.
	• Meals	• I had **breakfast** at 9 o'clock.
	• Proper nouns, such as languages, people and place names	• I'm learning **Chinese**. • I met **Liam** at the mall. • My cousins live in **Argentina**. • **Lake Superior** is the largest lake in **North America**. • They're going to climb **Mount Everest**.

EXCEPTIONS

- Use *the* with countries that have *of* in their name.
  The United States **of** America
  The Democratic People's Republic **of** Korea
- Use *the* with countries formed by groups of islands.
  The Maldives
  The Canary Islands
- Use *the* when the name of the country includes an institution.
  The Russian Federation
  The United Kingdom

Verbs: Simple Tenses

I **play** a lot of sports.

I **played** soccer last Saturday.

Tomorrow, I **will play** tennis with a friend.

4.1 Simple Present Tense

Every week, we **study** grammar in English class.

I **am** a secondary school student.

He **has** many books in his locker.

When do you use the simple present tense?

Use the simple present tense for the following situations:

1 A habit, routine or repeated action
   Simon **plays** hockey three nights a week.

2 A general truth or permanent action
   She **lives** in Paris.

3 Likes and dislikes
   Sarah **loves** the new hip hop artist.

4 Facts
   Smoking **causes** lung cancer.

5 A scheduled action in the future
   The exam **starts** at 9 a.m.

6 How a person feels; his or her state of mind
   I **feel** sick.   I **am** sad.

Time markers
Use these words and expressions to indicate the simple present tense.
• always, frequently, generally, never, often, rarely, seldom, sometimes, usually
• every second / minute / hour, every day / week / month / year
• in the morning / evening, on Mondays

How do you form the simple present tense?

Regular verbs

Follow these conjugation rules for most verbs.

	Simple present tense of the verb *walk*	
Affirmative	I walk You walk He / She / It walks He **walks** to school every day.	We walk You walk They walk
Negative	I do not (don't) walk You do not (don't) walk He / She / It does not (doesn't) walk We **do not** (**don't**) **walk** to school.	We do not (don't) walk You do not (don't) walk They do not (don't) walk
Interrogative	Do I walk? Do you walk? Does he / she / it walk? Do you **walk** to school? *Yes, I do. / No, I don't.*	Do we walk? Do you walk? Do they walk?
Tag question	Positive sentence—Negative tag They **walk** together, **don't** they? *Yes, they do. / No, they don't.* Negative sentence—Positive tag You **do not (don't) walk** to the park, **do** you? *Yes, I do. / No, I don't.*	

Third-person singular endings

Follow these rules for the third-person singular.

Rule	Examples
1 Add *s* to most verbs in the third-person singular.	add**s**, appreciate**s**, play**s**, practise**s**, work**s**
2 If the verb ends in *ch, o, s, sh, x* or *z*, add **es**.	buzz**es**, cross**es**, fix**es**, go**es**, wash**es**, watch**es**
3 If the verb ends in *y* preceded by a consonant, change the *y* to *ies*.	cr**ies**, l**ies**, sp**ies**, stud**ies**, tr**ies**

Irregular present tense verbs

The verbs *be* and *have* are irregular.

	Simple present tense of the verb *be*	Simple present tense of the verb *have*
Affirmative	I am (I'm) You are (You're) He / She / It is (He's / She's / It's) We are (We're) You are (You're) They are (They're) They **are** the best players on the team.	I have You have He / She / It has We have You have They have She **has** a red sports car.
Negative	I am (I'm) not You are not (aren't) He / She / It is not (isn't) We are not (aren't) You are not (aren't) They are not (aren't) I **am not** an elementary student. You **aren't** a football player.	I do not (don't) have You do not (don't) have He / She / It does not (doesn't) have We do not (don't) have You do not (don't) have They do not (don't) have You **do not have** iced tea in the fridge. We **don't have** money for the show.
Interrogative	Am I? Are you? Is he / she / it? Are we? Are you? Are they? **Are** you the new teacher? *Yes, I am. / No, I'm not.*	Do I have? Do you have? Does he / she / it have? Do we have? Do you have? Do they have? **Does** he **have** a cat? *Yes, he does. / No, he doesn't.*

	Simple present tense of the verb *be*	Simple present tense of the verb *have*
Tag question	Positive sentence—Negative tag We **are** young adults, **aren't** we? *Yes, we are. / No, we aren't.* Negative sentence—Positive tag You **are not** married, **are** you? *Yes, I am. / No, I'm not.*	Positive sentence—Negative tag You **have** two brothers, **don't** you? *Yes, I do. / No, I don't.* Negative sentence—Positive tag We **don't have** an exam, **do** we? *Yes, we do. / No, we don't.*

Note that you can also use *you're not*, *he's not*, and so on, as contractions for the negative simple present tense.

You**'re not** a football player.
He**'s not** the best player on the team, is he? – *No, he's not.*

BE CAREFUL!

The verb *be* does not need the auxiliary verb *do* in the simple present tense negative and interrogative forms.

Incorrect: ~~Does~~ she ~~is~~ the new student?

Correct: **Is** she the new student?

PRONUNCIATION

There are three ways to pronounce the *s* ending of third-person singular regular verbs.

/S/ sound for verbs ending in a *f, k, p, t* or *th* sound (unvoiced consonants)	/Z/ sound for verbs ending in a *b, d, g, l, m, n, ng, r, th, v* or *y* sound, (voiced consonants) or any vowel sound	/IZ/ sound for verbs ending in a *dg, s, sh, tch, x* or *z* sound
laughs, surfs	grabs	judges
likes, talks	lands	kisses
stops, wipes	hugs	pushes , catches
starts	breathes	fixes
creates	loves	chooses
unearths	plays	blazes

4.2 Simple Past Tense

I **played** soccer last Saturday.

My team **won** the championship game.

When do you use the simple past tense?

Use the simple past tense for the following situations:

1 Actions that began and ended at a specific time in the past
He **played** baseball with his friends last Sunday.

2 Actions that were often done in the past (habitual actions)
I often **visited** my family during the holidays.

3 A series of completed actions in the past
Abby **finished** her homework, and then she **walked** the dog.

Time markers
Use these words and expressions to indicate the simple past tense.
• after, before, during, earlier, then
• last night / week / month / year
• (two) seconds / minutes / hours / days / weeks / months / years ago
• yesterday, yesterday morning / afternoon
• a while back, once upon a time, when I was young

How do you form the simple past tense?

Regular verbs

To form the simple past tense, add **ed** to the base form of most verbs.

	Simple past tense of the verb *walk*	
Affirmative	I walked You walked He / She / It walked	We walked You walked They walked
	She **walked** to school when she was young.	
Negative	I did not (didn't) walk You did not (didn't) walk He / She / It did not (didn't) walk	We did not (didn't) walk You did not (didn't) walk They did not (didn't) walk
	Sean **did not** (**didn't**) **walk** to meet his friends.	

Simple past tense of the verb *walk*		
Interrogative	Did I walk? Did you walk? Did he / she / it walk? **Did** you **walk** to the restaurant? *Yes, I did. / No, I didn't.*	Did we walk? Did you walk? Did they walk?
Tag question	Positive sentence—Negative tag We **walked** together, **didn't** we? *Yes, we did. / No, we didn't.* Negative sentence—Positive tag You **did not** (**didn't**) **walk** to the park, **did** you? *Yes, I did. / No, I didn't.*	

Spelling rules

Follow these rules to form the simple past tense of regular verbs.

Rule	Examples
Add *ed* to most verbs.	answer**ed**, talk**ed**, visit**ed**, watch**ed**, work**ed**
If the verb ends in *a*, add *d* to the verb.	appreciate**d**, like**d**, practise**d**, receive**d**, use**d**
If the verb ends in *y* preceded by a consonant, change the *y* to *ied*.	appl**ied**, carr**ied**, cr**ied**, stud**ied**, tr**ied**
If the verb ends in *y* preceded by a vowel, keep the *y* and add *ed*.	play**ed**, stay**ed**
If the verb has one syllable and ends in a vowel and a consonant, **double the final consonant** and add *ed*.	drop**ped**, mop**ped**, plan**ned**, rub**bed**, stop**ped**
Exception: If the verb has two syllables and ends in a vowel and a consonant, and if the last syllable is stressed*, **double the final consonant** and add *ed*.	He ad**mitted** that he cheated on the exam. They re**ferred** to the dictionary.

* A stressed syllable is the syllable you emphasize when you say the word aloud. In the word *refer*, the stressed syllable is *fer* since you pronounce it more than the others.

PRONUNCIATION

There are three ways to pronounce the *ed* ending of regular verbs in the simple past tense.

/T/ sound for verbs ending in a *ch, f, k, p, s, sh, th* or *x* sound (unvoiced consonants)	/D/ sound for verbs ending with in a *b, g, l, m, n, r, th, v, w, y* or *z* sound (voiced consonants) or any vowel sound	/ID/ sound for verbs ending in a *d* or *t* sound
watched	robbed	added
laughed, surfed	hugged	decided
liked, talked	bathed	landed
stopped	loved	participated
unearthed	used	repeated
relaxed	vetoed	wanted

Irregular past tense verbs

Some verbs do not end in *ed* in the simple past tense. They are called irregular verbs. These verbs do not follow any specific rule. Here are a few examples:

take → took   eat → ate   forget → forgot

See page 125 for the Irregular Verbs Chart.

Two important irregular verbs are *be* and *have*.
The chart below shows how they are conjugated.

	Simple past tense of the verb *be*	Simple past tense of the verb *have*
Affirmative	I was You were He / She / It was We were You were They were	I had You had He / She / It had We had You had They had
	They **were** excited to see the movie.	She **had** a lot of homework.

	Simple past tense of the verb *be*	Simple past tense of the verb *have*
Negative	I was not (wasn't) You were not (weren't) He / She / It was not (wasn't) We were not (weren't) You were not (weren't) They were not (weren't) Ben **was not** happy with his grade. They **weren't** proud of themselves.	I did not (didn't) have You did not (didn't) have He / She / It did not (didn't) have We did not (didn't) have You did not (didn't) have They did not (didn't) have We **did not have** ice cream for dessert. Sarah **didn't have** her bicycle.
Interrogative	Was I? Were you? Was he / she / it? Were we? Were you? Were they? **Were** you surprised to see me? *Yes, I was. / No, I wasn't.*	Did I have? Did you have? Did he / she / it have? Did we have? Did you have? Did they have? **Did** she **have** french fries with her hot dog? *Yes, she did. / No, she didn't.*
Tag question	Positive sentence—Negative tag We **were** paid, **weren't** we? *Yes, we were. / No, we weren't.* Negative sentence—Positive tag You **were not** hurt, **were** you? *Yes, I was. / No, I wasn't.*	Positive sentence—Negative tag He **had** fun last night, **didn't** he? *Yes, he did. / No, he didn't.* Negative sentence—Positive tag We **didn't have** practice yesterday, **did** we? *Yes, we did. / No, we didn't.*

? MORE INFORMATION

The expression *used to* is in the simple past tense because it describes a habit, routine or past situation that is no longer relevant in the present.

She **used to** eat junk food every day, but now she only eats healthy food.

[4.3] Simple Future Tense

I **will finish** my homework tomorrow.

When do you use the simple future tense?

Use the simple future tense for the following situations:

1. Actions that will happen in the future
   Thomas **will attend** college in the fall.
2. Predictions about the future
   Madeline **will come** tomorrow.
3. Willingness (spontaneous decisions made at the moment of speaking)
   We really need another actor on the set. I **will call** Gabriel to see if he's interested.
4. Promises
   I promise that I **will pay** you back.

Time markers
Use these words and expressions to indicate the simple future tense:
• after, later, soon
• today, this evening, tonight
• tomorrow, tomorrow morning / afternoon / evening / night, the day after tomorrow
• next week / month / year / weekend
• next (day of the week) / (month of the year) / (season); next Friday / February / fall
• in (two) seconds / minutes / hours / days / weeks / months / years

How do you form the simple future tense?

Use the auxiliary *will* in front of any verb in its base form, including the verb *be*.

	Simple future tense with *will*	
Affirmative	I will (I'll) have You will (You'll) have He / She / It will (He'll / She'll / It'll) have	We will (We'll) have You will (You'll) have They will (They'll) have
	They **will have** a great time at the party this weekend.	

	Simple future tense with *will*	
Negative	I will not (won't) have You will not (won't) have He / She / It will not (won't) have	We will not (won't) have You will not (won't) have They will not (won't) have
	Drake **will not have** a new record deal. I **won't have** a hamburger for supper.	
Interrogative	Will I have? Will you have? Will he / she / it have?	Will we have? Will you have? Will they have?
	Will Mara **have** time for a bike ride? *Yes, she will. / No, she won't.*	
Tag question	Positive sentence—Negative tag You **will** have pie for dessert, **won't** you? *Yes, I will. / No, I won't.* Negative sentence—Positive tag We **won't** have a job tomorrow, **will** we? *Yes, we will. / No, we won't.*	

Notice that the main verb always stays in its base form.

They **will eat** spaghetti tonight.

? MORE INFORMATION

The use of *shall* is still found in formal English, but it is mostly a British expression. *Shall* is mainly used with the pronouns *I* and *we*.

I shall see you soon!
We shall meet again.

It is also used for suggestions.

Shall I close the window?
Shall we stop for lunch?

Future time with *be going to*

Be going to can also be used to express future time.
Be going to has essentially the same meaning as *will*.

See also the Simple Present Tense, page 18, and the Present Progressive Tense, page 32.

Use *be going to* in front of any verb in its base form, including the verb *be*.

	Future time with *be going to*
Affirmative	I am (I'm) going to play You are (You're) going to play He / She / It is (He's / She's / It's) going to play We are (We're) going to play You are (You're) going to play They are (They're) going to play Kristen **is going to play** the leading role.
Negative	I am (I'm) not going to play You are not (aren't) going to play He / She / It is not (isn't) going to play We are not (aren't) going to play You are not (aren't) going to play They are not (aren't) going to play Alex **isn't going to play** video games after his homework. He **isn't going to play** the violin for the crowd.
Interrogative	Am I going to play? Are we going to play? Are you going to play? Are you going to play? Is he / she / it going to play? Are they going to play? **Are** they **going to play** against the best team tonight?
Tag question	Positive sentence—Negative tag She **is going to play** tennis in the Olympics, **isn't** she? *Yes, she is. / No, she isn't.* Negative sentence—Positive tag They **aren't going to play** in the show, **are** they? *Yes, they are. / No, they aren't.*

Note that you can also use the contractions *you're not*, *he's not*, and so on, with *be going to* in the negative form.

He**'s not** going to play the violin.
They**'re not** going to play in the show.

BE CAREFUL!

The expression *gonna* is only used in informal speech and is unacceptable in written and formal English. It replaces *going to*.

Incorrect: He'**s** ~~**gonna dance**~~ all night.   Correct: He'**s going to dance** all night.

Will versus *be going to*

Sometimes, *will* and *be going to* have different meanings.

When to use *will*	When to use *be going to*
When we decide something spontaneously There's someone at the door. **I'll see** what he wants.	When an action is already planned in advance or is predicted to happen We **are going to travel** to Vancouver during March break. We'**re going to have** a great time.
When there is a condition If it rains, my friends and I **will rent** a movie. See Conditionals (first conditional), page 55.	When an action is about to happen. There is physical evidence that supports the prediction. Look out! The sculpture **is going to fall** over.

4.4 There Is / There Are

There is a dog in the backyard.

There are many people at the festival.

When do you use *there is / there are*?

In the simple present tense, use *there is* (and *there are* for the plural) to present a person, an animal or an object, usually in a specific place.

There is <u>a bear</u> in that tree. (*Is* agrees with "a bear.")
There are <u>many bears</u> in Canada. (*Are* agrees with "many bears.")

Note that the subject of the sentence is not *there* but the noun that follows the verb *be*. Be careful to conjugate the verb *be* in the correct tense: present, past or future.

There **were** no tickets left for the concert **yesterday**.
There **will be** a lot of people at the party **next Saturday**.

How do you form sentences with *there is / there are*?

Use this chart to help you form sentences using *there is / there are*.

		Singular	Plural
Present tense	Affirmative	There is (There's) **There is** a cat in the tree.	There are **There are** many good players on the team.
	Negative	There is not (There isn't) **There isn't** a cat in the tree.	There are not (There aren't) **There aren't** many good players on the team.
	Interrogative	Is there? **Is there** a cat in the tree?	Are there? **Are there** many good players on the team?
	Tag question	Positive sentence—Negative tag **There is** a cat in the tree, **isn't there?** *Yes, there is. / No, there isn't.* Negative sentence—Positive tag **There isn't** a raccoon in the tree, **is there?** *Yes, there is. / No, there isn't.*	Positive sentence—Negative tag **There are** many good players on the team, **aren't there?** *Yes, there are. / No, there aren't.* Negative sentence—Positive tag **There aren't** many teams in the area, **are there?** *Yes, there are. / No, there aren't.*
Past tense	Affirmative	There was **There was** a lot of traffic on the highway yesterday.	There were **There were** many people at the festival last weekend.
	Negative	There was not (There wasn't) **There was not** a lot of traffic on the highway.	There were not (There weren't) **There were not** many people at the festival last weekend.
	Interrogative	Was there? **Was there** a lot of traffic?	Were there? **Were there** many people?
	Tag question	Positive sentence—Negative tag **There was** a lot of traffic, **wasn't there?** *Yes, there was. / No, there wasn't.* Negative sentence—Positive tag **There wasn't** a lot of traffic, **was there?** *Yes, there was. / No, there wasn't.*	Positive sentence—Negative tag **There were** many people at the festival, **weren't there?** *Yes, there were. / No, there weren't.* Negative sentence—Positive tag **There weren't** many people at the festival, **were there?** *Yes, there were. / No, there weren't.*

		Singular	Plural
Future tense	Affirmative	There will be **There will be** plenty of food at the party.	There will be **There will be** many stars at the festival.
	Negative	There will not be (There won't be) **There will not be** much food at the party.	There will not be (There won't be) **There will not be** many stars at the festival.
	Interrogative	Will there be? **Will there be** any food at the party?	Will there be? **Will there be** many stars at the festival?
	Tag question	Positive sentence—Negative tag **There will be** plenty of food at the party, **won't there?** Negative sentence—Positive tag **There won't be** much food, **will there?**	Positive sentence—Negative tag **There will be** many people, **won't there?** Negative sentence—Positive tag **There won't be** many people, **will there?**

Be going to can also be used with *there is* and *there are* to express future continuous time when talking about planned events and predictions. Use *be going to* instead of *will*.

Affirmative   **There is going to be** plenty of food at the party.
                  There are going to be many stars at the festival.

Negative   **There is not going to be** much food at the party.
                  There are not going to be many stars at the festival.

Interrogative   **Is there going to be** any food at the party?
                  Are there going to be many stars at the festival?

Tag question   **There is going to be** plenty of food at the party, **isn't there?**
                  There isn't going to be much food at the party, **is there?**
                  There are going to be many people, **aren't there?**
                  There aren't going to be many people, **are there?**

Unit 5

Verbs: Progressive Tenses

Aisha **is eating** her breakfast.

Yesterday, she **was studying** from 6 p.m. to 9 p.m.

She **will be skiing** in the Alps during the holidays.

5.1 Present Progressive Tense

Emma **is playing** with her ball.

When do you use the present progressive tense?

Use the present progressive tense for the following situations:

1. Actions that are happening at the moment
   Look, the neighbours **are moving** out of their house.

2. Actions that are happening during this period of time and are temporary
   Gabrielle **is** currently **living** in Toronto.
   I **am learning** Chinese.

3. An irritation, something that is bothersome
   My sister **is** always **taking** my CDs.

4. A definite future event, a fixed future arrangement
   Our teacher **is meeting** with us **at** 10 a.m.

> **MORE INFORMATION**
>
> The progressive tenses are also called the continuous tenses.

Time markers
Use these words and expressions to indicate the present progressive tense.
• at the moment, currently, now, presently, right now
• this morning / afternoon / evening / week / year
• today, at (exact time), in (minutes, hours, days, weeks)
• always, soon

How do you form the present progressive tense?

Follow these rules to form the present progressive tense.

	Present progressive tense of the verb *walk*	
Affirmative	I am (I'm) walking You are (You're) walking He / She / It is (He's / She's / It's) walking	We are (We're) walking You are (You're) walking They are (They're) walking
	You **are** (You**'re**) **walking** outside without a hat.	
Negative	I am not (I'm not) walking You are not (aren't) walking He / She / It is not (isn't) walking	We are not (aren't) walking You are not (aren't) walking They are not (aren't) walking
	You **are not (aren't) walking** very fast.	
Interrogative	Am I walking? Are you walking? Is he / she / it walking?	Are we walking? Are you walking? Are they walking?
	Is Paul **walking** to the station? *Yes, he is. / No, he isn't.*	
Tag questions	Positive sentence—Negative tag Sean **is walking** on the football field, **isn't** he? *Yes, he is. / No, he isn't.*	
	Negative sentence—Positive tag They **are not (aren't) walking** to school today, **are** they? *Yes, they are. / No, they aren't.*	

Remember to conjugate the verb *be* in the simple present tense.

See Simple Present Tense, page 18.

Note that you can also use *you're not*, *he's not*, and so on, as contractions for the negative simple present tense.

He**'s not walking** very fast.
They**'re not walking** to school today, **are** they? *No, they're not.*

Spelling rules for the *ing* verb

The base form of a verb ending in *ing* is called a present participle.

Rule	Examples
Add *ing* to the end of the base form of most verbs.	cook**ing**, play**ing**, sleep**ing**, study**ing**, work**ing**
If the verb ends in *e*, delete the *e* and add *ing*.	bicycl**ing**, chas**ing**, dat**ing**, participat**ing**, rid**ing**
If the verb ends in *ie*, change the *ie* to **y** and add *ing*.	d**ying**, l**ying**
If a verb has one syllable and ends in a vowel and a consonant, double the consonant and add *ing*.	beg**ging**, plan**ning**, stop**ping**
If a verb has two syllables and ends in a vowel and a consonant, • if the first syllable is stressed, add *ing*; • if the second syllable is stressed, double the consonant and add *ing*.	<u>lis</u>ten**ing**, <u>of</u>fering be<u>gin</u>**ning**, con<u>trol</u>**ling**, pre<u>fer</u>**ring**

The present progressive tense versus the simple present tense

Use this chart to compare the present progressive tense with the simple present tense.

Present progressive tense	Simple present tense
• Used for temporary actions or actions that are in progress • Used for actions happening right now They **are working** right now.	• Used for permanent actions • Used for habits, usual actions They **work** from Monday to Friday.
• Uses the verb *be* for all the affirmative, negative and interrogative forms **Are** you **watching** television? We **are not watching** television at the moment.	• Uses *do* or *does* in the negative and interrogative forms (for all verbs except *be* and modal auxiliaries) ⬇ See Modal Auxiliaries, page 51. **Do** you watch much television? We **don't watch** much television.
• Used with action verbs only He **is playing** baseball. (action verb) He ~~is seeming~~ happy. (non-action verb)	• Used with action and non-action verbs He **plays** baseball every Friday. (action verb) He **seems** happy today. (non-action verb)

What are non-action verbs?

Non-action verbs, also called stative verbs, express state, sense, desire, possession or opinion. No action occurs when you use them, and they cannot be used in the present progressive tense.

Incorrect: I ~~am believing~~ in you.   Correct: I **believe** in you.

Here is a list of non-action verbs.

admire	contain	imagine	prefer
amaze	cost	impress	promise
appear	depend	know	resemble
appreciate	deserve	love	seem
astonish	desire	matter	smell
be	(dis)agree	mean	suppose
believe	(dis)like	mind	surprise
belong	fit	need	taste
care	forget	owe	think
concern	hate	own	understand
consider	have	please	want
consist	hear	possess	wish

Some verbs can act as non-action *and* action verbs depending on how they are used in a sentence.

She **has** an old car. (possession—non-action)
She **is having** car problems. (experience—action)

He **is** selfish. (state—non-action)
He **is being** selfish. (present behaviour—action)

I **think** it's a great idea. (opinion—non-action)
I **am thinking** about your suggestion. (consideration—action)

[5.2] Past Progressive Tense

> Owen **was studying** when his friend called him.

When do you use the past progressive tense?

Use the past progressive tense for the following situations:

1 Actions in progress at a specific moment in the past
Joshua **was repairing** his car from 9 a.m. to 3 p.m. yesterday.

2 Simultaneous actions happening in the past
Nathalie **was listening** to music while she **was studying** math.

3 Gradual development
The sun **was setting** slowly on the horizon.

4 Annoying actions (with *always, constantly*)
He **was** constantly **complaining**!

5 Interrupted actions
Pina **was walking** outside when it began to rain
(and interrupted Pina walking).

Time markers
Use these words to indicate the past progressive tense.
• as, still, when, while
• always, constantly, forever
• last night / week / month / year, yesterday

When versus *while* and *as*

When and *while* are used in sentences to indicate interrupted actions:

Past progressive tense + *when* + simple past tense

See Simple Past Tense, page 22.

interrupted action   interrupting action
We **were playing** soccer **when** the bell **rang**.

While + past progressive tense + simple past tense
          interrupted action   interrupting action
While we **were playing** soccer, the bell **rang**.

Use *as* with the past progressive tense to indicate *during the process*.

I banged my head **as I was getting out of the car**.

Use *while* with the past progressive tense to indicate a simultaneous action.

Nathan was cleaning his room **while Sophie was preparing dinner**.

How do you form the past progressive tense?

Follow these rules to form the past progressive tense. See Present Progressive Tense, page 34, for rules on the *ing* form.

	Past progressive tense of the verb *walk*	
Affirmative	I was walking You were walking He / She / It was walking Daisy **was walking** in the park.	We were walking You were walking They were walking
Negative	I was not (wasn't) walking You were not (weren't) walking He / She / It was not (wasn't) walking Robby and Olivia **were not (weren't) walking** to the sports centre.	We were not (weren't) walking You were not (weren't) walking They were not (weren't) walking
Interrogative	Was I walking? Were you walking? Was he / she / it walking? **Were** they **walking** toward the lake? *Yes, they were. / No, they weren't.*	Were we walking? Were you walking? Were they walking?
Tag questions	Positive sentence—Negative tag Adèle **was walking** fast, **wasn't** she? *Yes, she was. / No, she wasn't.* Negative sentence—Positive tag Noah **wasn't walking** on the sidewalk, **was** he? *Yes, he was. / No, he wasn't.*	

Note that non-action verbs cannot be used in the past progressive tense.

Incorrect: You ~~were promising~~ me.

Correct: You **promised** me.

See Present Progressive Tense, page 35, for a list of non-action verbs.

⌈5.3⌉ Future Progressive Tense

> **I will be skiing** in the Alps during the winter holidays.

When do you use the future progressive tense?

Use the future progressive tense for the following situations:

1 Actions that will be in progress in the future
William **will be cleaning** his room all morning.

2 Actions that are scheduled to happen
She **will be arriving** at 5 p.m.

3 Predictions
You **will be selling** your house and **moving** far away.

4 Simultaneous actions
Bruno **will be cooking** while Catherine **will be playing** with the kids.

5 Interrupted actions in the future
My brothers **will be watching** a movie when I arrive from school
(and interrupt them).

Note the tenses used:

future progressive tense + simple present tense ⊢─── ↑ See Simple Present Tense, page 18.

           interrupted action   interrupting action

My brothers **will be watching** a movie when I **arrive** from school.

Time markers
Use these words to indicate the future progressive tense.
• today, tonight, tomorrow, next week / month / year, this week / month / year
• in (two) days / weeks / months / years
• as, at this time, before, during, still, soon, when, while

How do you form the future progressive tense?

Follow these rules to form the future progressive tense. ⊢ ↑ See Present Progressive Tense, page 34, for rules on the *ing* form

	Future progressive tense of the verb *walk*	
Affirmative	I will (I'll) be walking You will (You'll) be walking He / She / It will (He'll / She'll / It'll) be walking	We will (We'll) be walking You will (You'll) be walking They will (They'll) be walking
	Next week, we **will** (we'**ll**) **be walking** in Paris.	

	Future progressive tense of the verb *walk*	
Negative	I will not (won't) be walking You will not (won't) be walking He / She / It will not (won't) be walking	We will not (won't) be walking You will not (won't) be walking They will not (won't) be walking
	The teacher **will not** (**won't**) **be walking** to school today.	
Interrogative	Will I be walking? Will you be walking? Will he / she / it be walking?	Will we be walking? Will you be walking? Will they be walking?
	Will she **be walking** to the ice cream shop after dinner? *Yes, she will. / No, she will not (won't).*	
Tag question	Positive sentence—Negative tag The actors **will be walking** the red carpet, **won't** they? *Yes, they will. / No, they won't.* Negative sentence—Positive tag The actors **won't be walking** the red carpet, **will** they? *Yes, they will. / No, they won't.*	

Note that non-action verbs cannot be used in the future progressive tense.

Incorrect: He ~~will be loving~~ me.   Correct: He **will love** me.

See Present Progressive Tense, page 35, for a list of non-action verbs.

Future progressive with *be going to*

Be going to can also be used to express future continuous time when talking about planned events and predictions. Use *be going to* instead of *will*.

	Future progressive tense with *be going to*
Affirmative	**They are going to be flying** to Paris soon.
Negative	The teacher **is not (isn't) going to be leaving** on time today.
Interrogative	**Is** Rachel **going to be** leaving school this year?
Tag question	Positive sentence––Negative tag The singer **is going to be leaving soon, isn't** he? *Yes, he is. / No, he isn't.* Negative sentence––Positive tag The singer **isn't going to be leaving for a while, is** he? *Yes, he is. / No, he isn't.*

Verbs: Perfect Tenses

Kristen **has been** at this school for four years.

I **hadn't met** Aiden until yesterday.

He **will have finished** his homework by 9 p.m.

She **has been playing** the drums for two years.

I **had been looking** for my cat all afternoon when I saw it in a tree.

We **will have been seeing** each other for six months next weekend.

6.1 Present Perfect Tense

Charlie **has worked** for his company since 1992.

When do you use the present perfect tense?

Use the present perfect tense for the following situations:

1 Actions that started in the past and continue in the present
I **have lived** in Toronto for three years.
The Johnson family **has** never **visited** the Toronto Zoo (in their lives).

2 Repeated actions that happened before now (and may be repeated again)
We **have played** this video game many times.

3 Past actions that happened at an unspecified moment, whether because the time is unknown or because it is unimportant
I**'ve mailed** my application.

4️⃣ Actions that take place during an incomplete period of time
I **have jogged** five kilometres so far.

5️⃣ News of recent events, recent actions
The company **has** just **closed** its doors.

Time markers
Use these words and expressions to indicate the present perfect tense.
• already, before, just, lately, many times, never, occasionally, often, once, recently, sometimes
• ever, yet (with questions and negative form)
• for (a period of time), since (a specific time)
• today, this week / month / year, so far, up to now

How do you form the present perfect tense?

See Simple Present Tense, page 20, for the complete conjugation of the verb *have*.

The present perfect tense is formed using
subject + simple present tense of *have* + past participle of the main verb.

	Present perfect tense of the verb *visit*	
Affirmative	I have (I've) visited You have (You've) visited He / She / It has (She's / He's / It's) visited	We have (We've) visited You have (You've) visited They have (They've) visited
	Lucy **has visited** her grandmother many times recently.	
Negative	I have not (haven't) visited You have not (haven't) visited He / She / It has not (hasn't) visited	We have not (haven't) visited You have not (haven't) visited They have not (haven't) visited
	We **have not (haven't) visited** Europe yet.	
Interrogative	Have I visited? Have you visited? Has he / she / it visited?	Have we visited? Have you visited? Have they visited?
	Have the students **visited** their sick friend? *Yes, they have. / No, they haven't.*	
Tag questions	Positive sentence—Negative tag Sarah **has visited** her friend a lot lately, **hasn't** she? *Yes, she has. / No, she hasn't.* Negative sentence—Positive tag The new owners **have not (haven't) visited** their house yet, **have** they? *Yes, they have. / No, they haven't.*	

Past participle

Regular verbs: the past participle has the same spelling as the simple past tense.

liked   played   planned   studied   walked

See Simple Tenses, page 23, for spelling rules for regular verbs.

Irregular verbs: the past participle is listed in the **third column** of the Irregular Verbs Chart on page 125.

eaten   gone   kept   seen   written

For and *since*

Note the difference in the way you use *for* and *since* with the present perfect tense.

For	Since
Use for periods of time, duration (number of seconds, minutes, hours, years, decades, centuries). I've known him **for five months**.	Use with specific moments in the past (days of the week, months of the year, time, date, holidays or special days). I've known him **since September**.

Present perfect tense versus simple past tense

Use this chart to compare the present perfect tense with the simple past tense.

Present perfect tense	Simple past tense
Actions that started in the past and continue in the present Ariadna **has studied** English for two months.	Finished actions Ariadna **received** her final grade in English last week, and she **passed**.
Repeated actions that happened before now (and may be repeated again) He **has done** this puzzle many times.	Chronological actions in the past He **worked** on the puzzle for three hours, and finally he **finished** it.
Past actions that happened at a moment that is unspecified, either because the moment is unknown or because it is unimportant They **have** already **met**.	Actions that happened at specific moments in the past They **met** at the movies last Friday.
Actions that take place during an incomplete period of time I **haven't visited** London this year. I **have visited** London a lot this year.	Actions that happened during a completed period of time in the past When I was in London, I **saw** Buckingham Palace and I **walked** along the River Thames.
News of recent events or actions Beth **has had** an accident.	Finished actions She **fell** on the ice during practice and **broke** her arm.

6.2 Past Perfect Tense

> Before the film ended, Thomas **had fallen** asleep.

When do you use the past perfect tense?

Use the past perfect tense to express an action that happened before another past action or point in time.

Note that the action that happens *first* is in the past perfect tense; the action that happens *second* is in the simple past tense.

first action   second action

Sam **had cooked** dinner by the time Megan **arrived** home from work. See Simple Past Tense, page 22.

Time markers
Use these words and expressions to indicate the past perfect tense.
• already, just
• after, before, so, until, when
• by the time, by then, up to that time

How do you form the past perfect tense?

The past perfect tense is formed using subject + *had* + past participle of the main verb. See Past Participle, page 42.

Past perfect tense of the verb *plan*		
Affirmative	I had (I'd) planned You had (You'd) planned He / She / It had (He'd / She'd / It'd) planned	We had (We'd) planned You had (You'd) planned They had (They'd) planned
	My brother **had planned** his trip before the accident.	
Negative	I had not (hadn't) planned You had not (hadn't) planned He / She / It had not (hadn't) planned	We had not (hadn't) planned You had not (hadn't) planned They had not (hadn't) planned
	Our boss **had not (hadn't) planned** the meeting.	
Interrogative	Had I planned? Had you planned? Had he / she / it planned?	Had we planned? Had you planned? Had they planned?
	Had your mother already **planned** the dinner menu? *Yes, she had. / No, she hadn't.*	

	Past perfect tense of the verb *plan*
Tag questions	Positive sentence—Negative tag Danny **had planned** his vacation in detail, **hadn't** he? *Yes, he had. / No, he hadn't.* Negative sentence—Positive tag William and David **hadn't planned** to drive, **had** they? *Yes, they had. / No, they hadn't.*

[6.3] Future Perfect Tense

Sonia **will have corrected** the students' exams *by* next week.

When do you use the future perfect tense?

Use the future perfect tense for the following situations:

1 An action in the future preceding another action in the future

The train **will have** already **left** when you arrive at the station.

2 Duration of an action preceding another action in the future

By the time I leave, I **will have worked** here for five years.

Note that the action that happens *first* or is *completed* is in the future perfect tense; the action that happens *second* is in the simple present tense.

first action   second action

Isabelle **will have finished** her supper by the time you **get** here.

See Simple Present Tense, page 18.

Time markers
Use these words and expressions to indicate the future perfect tense.
• already
• for (period of time)
• before, by (a certain time), by the time, when

How do you form the future perfect tense?

The future perfect tense is formed using
subject + *will have* + past participle of the main verb.

See Past Participle, page 42.

	Future perfect tense of the verb *practise*	
Affirmative	I will (I'll) have practised You will (You'll) have practised He/She/It will (He'll/She'll/It'll) have practised	We will (We'll) have practised You will (You'll) have practised They will (They'll) have practised
	Cathy **will have practised** the piano when you arrive.	
Negative	I will not (won't) have practised You will not (won't) have practised He/She/It will not (won't) have practised	We will not (won't) have practised You will not (won't) have practised They will not (won't) have practised
	Max **will not (won't) have** practised Japanese before leaving for Japan.	
Interrogative	Will I have practised? Will you have practised? Will he/she/it have practised?	Will we have practised? Will you have practised? Will they have practised?
	Will Vicky **have** practised her dance before the bell rings? *Yes, she will. / No, she won't.*	
Tag questions	Positive sentence—Negative tag They **will have practised** during their lunch break, **won't** they? *Yes, they will. / No, they won't.* Negative sentence—Positive tag Jon **will not (won't) have practised** his lines, **will** he? *Yes, he will. / No, he won't.*	

Future perfect tense with *be going to*

Be going to can also be used with the future perfect tense when talking about planned events and predictions.

Use *be going to* instead of *will*. See Simple Future Tense, page 26.

	Future perfect tense with *be going to*	
Affirmative	Scott **is going to have finished** the project by the time we arrive.	
Negative	John and Cameron **are not going to have learned** the song in time for the concert.	
Interrogative	**Is** Zoe **going to have read** the book before English class?	
Tag questions	Positive sentence—Negative tag We**'re going to have missed** the start of the movie, **aren't** we? *Yes, we are. / No, we aren't.* Negative sentence—Positive tag We**'re not going to have missed** much, **are** we? *Yes, we are. / No, we aren't.*	

6.4 Present Perfect Progressive Tense

Alexis **has been babysitting** the neighbours' children all weekend.

When do you use the present perfect progressive tense?

Use the present perfect progressive tense to express the duration of an action that started in the past and is still going on in the present.

We **have been living** in Ottawa for a year and we love it!

Time markers
Use these words and expressions to indicate the present perfect progressive tense.
• lately, now, recently
• for (a period of time), since (a specific time) See *For* and *since*, page 42.
• all (morning / afternoon / day / night / week / weekend / month / year)

? MORE INFORMATION

The progressive tenses are also called the continuous tenses.

How do you form the present perfect progressive tense?

The present perfect progressive tense is formed using subject + present perfect of *be* + present participle of the main verb. See Present Progressive Tense, page 34, for spelling rules.

Present perfect progressive tense of the verb *teach*		
Affirmative	I have (I've) been teaching You have (You've) been teaching He / She / It has (He's / She's / It's) been teaching	We have (We've) been teaching You have (You've) been teaching They have (They've) been teaching
	Annie **has been teaching** dancing for two years now.	
Negative	I have not (haven't) been teaching You have not (haven't) been teaching He / She / It has not (hasn't) been teaching	We have not (haven't) been teaching You have not (haven't) been teaching They have not (haven't) been teaching
	Miha **has not (hasn't) been teaching** art for very long.	

Present perfect progressive tense of the verb *teach*		
Interrogative	Have I been teaching? Have you been teaching? Has he/she/it been teaching? **Have** James and Imami **been teaching** the song to the group? *Yes, they have. / No, they haven't.*	Have we been teaching? Have you been teaching? Have they been teaching?
Tag questions	Positive sentence—Negative tag The construction workers **have been teaching** the new guy for months now, **haven't** they? *Yes, they have. / No, they haven't.* Negative sentence—Positive tag Grandpa **hasn't been teaching** his old dog new tricks, **has** he? *Yes, he has. / No, he hasn't.*	

Note that non-action verbs cannot be used in the progressive tenses.

Incorrect: I ~~have been knowing~~ him for six years.

Correct: I **have known** him for six years.

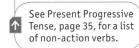
See Present Progressive Tense, page 35, for a list of non-action verbs.

[6.5] Past Perfect Progressive Tense

Will and Harry **had been talking** for over an hour before Eli arrived.

When do you use the past perfect progressive tense?

Use the past perfect progressive tense to express a continuous action that started in the past and was completed or interrupted at some point in the past.

Note that the action that is *interrupted* is in the past perfect progressive tense; the *interrupting* action is in the simple past tense.

interrupted action   interrupting action

I **had been cycling** all afternoon when I **got** a flat tire.

Time markers
Use these words and expressions to indicate the past perfect progressive tense.
• for (a period of time), since (a specific time)
• all (morning/afternoon/evening/night/week/weekend/month/year)
• before, when

How do you form the past perfect progressive tense?

The past perfect progressive tense is formed using
subject + past perfect of *be* + present participle of the main verb.

See Present Progressive Tense, page 34, for spelling rules.

	Past perfect progressive tense of the verb *train*	
Affirmative	I had (I'd) been training You had (You'd) been training He/She/It had (He'd/She'd/It'd) been training	We had (We'd) been training You had (You'd) been training They had (They'd) been training
	He **had (He'd) been training** for a year before the competition.	
Negative	I had not (hadn't) been training You had not (hadn't) been training He/She/It had not (hadn't) been training	We had not (hadn't) been training You had not (hadn't) been training They had not (hadn't) been training
	They **had not (hadn't) been training** for over a month.	
Interrogative	Had I been training? Had you been training? Had he/she/it been training? **Had** Chad **been training** all day? *Yes, he had. / No, he hadn't.*	Had we been training? Had you been training? Had they been training?
Tag questions	Positive sentence—Negative tag Maude **had been training** for the big game, **hadn't** she? *Yes, she had. / No, she hadn't.* Negative sentence—Positive tag Casey **hadn't been training** the new employee, **had** she? *Yes, she had. / No, she hadn't.*	

Note that non-action verbs cannot be used in the progressive tenses.

Incorrect: I ~~had been owning~~ the guitar for six years.

Correct: I **had owned** the guitar for six years.

See Present Progressive Tense, page 35, for a list of non-action verbs.

6.6 Future Perfect Progressive Tense

She **will have been studying** for four years by the time she graduates.

When do you use the future perfect progressive tense?

Use the future perfect progressive tense for the following situations:

1 Actions that will be in progress in the future

In a week's time, we **will have been going out** for six months.

2 Actions that will continue up until they are interrupted in the future

We **will have been working** for hours by the time Mika arrives.

Note that the action that is *interrupted* is in the future perfect progressive tense; the *interrupting* action is in the simple present tense.

interrupted action   interrupting action

Eric **will have been teaching** for a year by the time he **leaves** the school.

See Present Progressive Tense, page 34, for spelling rules.

Time markers
Use these words and expressions to indicate the future perfect progressive tense.
• already, for (a period of time)
• because, before, by the time, when

How do you form the future perfect progressive tense?

The future perfect progressive tense is formed using
subject + *will have been* + present participle of the main verb.

	Future perfect progressive tense of the verb *talk*	
Affirmative	I will (I'll) have been talking You will (You'll) have been talking He / She / It will (He'll / She'll / It'll) have been talking	We will (We'll) have been talking You will (You'll) have been talking They will (They'll) have been talking
	Mr. Davis **will have been talking** to his students for an hour.	
Negative	I will not (won't) have been talking You will not (won't) have been talking He / She / It will not (won't) have been talking	We will not (won't) have been talking You will not (won't) have been talking They will not (won't) have been talking
	They **will not (won't) have been talking** for hours in that meeting.	

	Future perfect progressive tense of the verb *talk*	
Interrogative	Will I have been talking? Will you have been talking? Will he/she/it have been talking? **Will** they **have been talking** all night? *Yes, they will. / No, they won't.*	Will we have been talking? Will you have been talking? Will they have been talking?
Tag question	Positive sentence—Negative tag Hannah **will have been talking** to her friend all morning, **won't** she? *Yes, she will. No, she won't.* Negative sentence—Positive tag Hannah **will not (won't) have been talking** to her friend all morning, **will** she? *Yes, she will. No, she won't.*	

↑ See Simple Future Tense, page 26, for the contracted form of *will*.

Note that non-action verbs cannot be used in the progressive tenses.

Incorrect: I ~~will have been belonging~~ to the club for two years.

Correct: I **will have belonged** to the club for two years.

↑ See Present Progressive Tense, page 35, for a list of non-action verbs.

Future perfect progressive tense with *be going to*

Be going to can also be used with the future perfect progressive tense when talking about planned events and predictions.

Use *be going to* instead of *will*.

	Future perfect progressive tense with *be going to*
Affirmative	Mr. Davis **is going to have been talking** to his students for an hour.
Negative	They **are not (aren't) going to have been talking** for hours in that meeting.
Interrogative	**Are** they **going to have been talking** all night? *Yes, they are. / No, they aren't.*
Tag questions	Positive sentence—Negative tag Hannah **is going to have been talking** to her friend all morning, **isn't** she? *Yes, she is. / No, she isn't.* Negative sentence—Positive tag Hannah **is not (isn't) going to have been talking** to her friend all morning, **is** she? *Yes, she is. / No, she isn't.*

Unit 7

Modal Auxiliaries and Conditionals

I **must** get a job.
If I **don't get** a job, I **won't have** enough money to travel.

[7.1] Modal Auxiliaries

You **must** stop at the traffic light .

What are modals?

Modals are auxiliaries that are used with verbs in their base form and which add another meaning to the sentence. Most modal auxiliaries have more than one meaning.

How do you use modals?

Common modals are used for the following functions:

1 Ability

Alex **can** ride a bike.
Sunita **could** run a marathon last year.

2 Advisability

You **should** call her.
You **ought to** call her.

3 Expectation

You **should** pass the test—you have worked hard.

4 Future actions

I **will** talk to her tomorrow. ↑ See Simple Future Tense, page 26.

5 Logical conclusion

Harriet **must** be home by now.

That **can't** be Noah's sister—she's too tall.

6 Obligation / Necessity

We **must** follow the rules.

We **have to** leave now.

7 Past routine

They **would** often play together in elementary school.

8 Permission

Can I ride your bike?

Could we use your phone?

May I sit here?

9 Polite request

Can you open the door, please?

Could you help me, please?

Would you wait here, please?

10 Possibility

Volcanoes **can** erupt any time.

He **can't** be home yet—he only just left.

He **could** win.

It **may** rain today.

We **might** be wrong.

11 Prediction

Your father **will** be fine.

I **shall** see you tonight. (Rarely used in North America)

12 Prohibition

You **mustn't** be late.

How do you form modal auxiliaries?

Here is how to use modals in a sentence:

Subject + **modal** + **base form of the verb** + complement

Alex **can ride** a bike.

This chart shows how to form the different modals.

Modal	Function	Affirmative	Negative	Interrogative
can	Ability	Alex **can** ride a bike.	Alex **cannot** (**can't**) ride a bike.	**Can** Alex ride a bike?
	Permission	You **can** ride my bike.	You **can't** ride my bike.	**Can** I ride your bike?
	Polite request			**Can** you open the door, please?
	Possibility	Volcanoes **can** erupt any time.	Volcanoes **cannot** (**can't**) erupt any time.	**Can** volcanoes erupt any time?
	Logical conclusion	That **can't** be Noah's sister—she's too tall.		
could	Past ability	She **could** run a marathon last year.	She **could not** (**couldn't**) run a marathon last year.	**Could** she run a marathon last year?
	Permission			**Could** we use your phone?
	Possibility	He **could** win.	He **could not** (**couldn't**) win.	**Could** he win?
	Polite request			**Could** you help me, please?
may	Possibility	It **may** rain today.	It **may not** rain today.	
	Permission	You **may** sit here.	You **may not** sit here.	**May** I sit here?
might	Possibility	We **might** be wrong.	We **might not** be wrong.	**Might** we be wrong?
must	Logical conclusion	She **must** be home by now.		
	Obligation	We **must** follow the rules.		**Must** we follow the rules?
	Prohibition		You **must not** (**mustn't**) be late.	
have to	Obligation / Necessity	We **have to** leave now.	We **do not** (**don't**) **have to** leave now.	**Do** we **have to** leave now?

Modal Auxiliaries and Conditionals

Modal	Function	Affirmative	Negative	Interrogative
should	Advisability	You **should** call her.	You **should not** (**shouldn't**) call her.	**Should** I call her?
	Expectation	You **should** pass the test.	You **should not** (**shouldn't**) fail the test.	**Should** I pass the test?
ought to	Advisability	He **ought to** call her.	He **ought not to** call her.	**Ought** he **to** call her?
shall	Prediction	I **shall** see you tonight.	I **shall not** (**shan't**) see you tonight.	**Shall** I see you tonight?
will	Prediction	Your father **will** be fine.	Your father **will not** (**won't**) be fine.	**Will** our father be fine?
	Future actions	I **will** (**I'll**) talk to her tomorrow.	I **will not** (**won't**) talk to her tomorrow.	**Will** you talk to her tomorrow?
would	Polite request			**Would** you wait here, please?
	Past routine	They **would** often play together.	They **would not** (**wouldn't**) often play together.	**Would** they often play together?

BE CAREFUL!

- Do not contract the negative form of *may*.
  Incorrect: He ~~mayn't~~ go on the trip.
  Correct: He **may not** go on the trip.
- *May* is not used in the interrogative form when talking about possibility.
  Incorrect: ~~May~~ it rain tonight?
  Correct: **Will i**t rain tonight?
- When expressing an obligation in the past tense, use *have to*.
  Incorrect: Yesterday, I ~~must~~ return my books.
  Correct: Yesterday, I **had to** return my books.
- Remember that *have to* can be used in the present, past and future tenses.
  Maya **has to** / **had to** / **will have to** work all night.
- When expressing ability in past and future tenses, use either *can* or *be able to*.
  I **can** help you tomorrow.
  I **will be able to** help you tomorrow.

7.2 Conditional Sentences

> **If** Sabrina **is** late again, she **will be** in trouble.
>
> **If** Sabrina **got up** earlier, she **would catch** the bus.
>
> **If** she **had been** on time, she **would have heard** the news.

Conditional sentences describe an action and its results. Conditional sentences have two parts: the *if* **clause** (condition) and the **result clause** (independent clause).

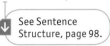

See Sentence Structure, page 98.

When do you use conditional sentences?

1 First conditional: present real conditions

Use a first conditional sentence when the condition and the result are real or possible in the present or future.

If you **take** driving lessons, you **will get** your license.

2 Second conditional: present or future unreal conditions

Use a second conditional sentence when you talk about an unreal or improbable situation in the present or future.

If Peter **practised**, he **would be** a great player. (Real situation: he doesn't practise.)

3 Third conditional: past unreal conditions

Use a third conditional sentence when you talk about a past unreal situation. Neither the condition nor the result ever happened, so the situation is hypothetical.

If Leah **had gone** on the trip, she **would have seen** the Grand Canyon. (Real situation: she didn't go on the trip.)

How do you form conditional sentences?

Use this chart to help you form conditional sentences.

First conditional	*If* clause	Result clause
	Simple present tense	Simple future tense
Affirmative	If I **win** the lottery,	I **will travel** around the world.
Negative	If I **do not (don't) win** the lottery,	I **will not (won't) travel** around the world.
	If I **win** the lottery, If I **don't win** the lottery,	I **won't travel** … I **will travel** …
Interrogative	If I **do not (don't) study** very hard,	**will I get** better grades?

	If clause	Result clause
Second conditional	**Simple past tense**	***Would* + main verb**
Affirmative	If we **had** the money, If they **were** here,	we **would travel** around the world. they **would help** you.
Negative	If we **did not (didn't) have** the money, If they **were not (weren't)** here,	we **would not (wouldn't) travel** around the world. they **would not (wouldn't) help** you.
Interrogative	If we **had** the money,	**would** we **travel** around the world?
Third conditional	**Past perfect tense**	***Would have* + past participle of main verb**
Affirmative	If Ashley **had planned** her weekend in advance,	she **would have spent** it with her friends.
Negative	If Ashley **had not planned** her weekend in advance,	she **would not have spent** it with her friends.
Interrogative	If Ashley **had not (hadn't) planned** her weekend in advance,	**would** she **have spent** it with her friends?

Note that the *if* clause can be placed before or after the result clause.

See Past participle, page 42.

If it rains, I will bring an umbrella.
I will bring an umbrella **if it rains**.

If the *if* clause comes before the result clause, the clauses are separated by a comma.

❋ EXCEPTIONS

First conditional:

• When expressing automatic results (*if* = *every time, whenever*), put the result clause in the simple present tense, not the future tense.
  If (= *whenever*) I drive through a red light, I **break** the law.

• When expressing an order or a suggestion, put the result clause in the imperative form.
See Imperative Sentences, page 7.
  If you like the outdoors, **go** camping in the Adirondacks.

Second conditional:

• With the verb *be*, use ***were*** for all persons in the *if* clause, singular and plural.
  If I **were** a millionaire, I would give a lot of money to charity.

  Informally, ***was*** can be used for first-person and third-person singular.

  If I **was** a millionaire, I would give a lot of money to charity.
  If he **was** a millionaire, he would give a lot of money to charity.

Modals in conditional sentences

Use modals in the result clause of a conditional sentence to express possibility or permission.

	If clause	Result clause
First conditional	**Simple present tense**	**Modal + main verb**
	If they **work** hard this year,	they **might receive** a raise.
Second conditional	**Simple past tense**	**Modal + main verb**
	If he **applied** for the job,	he **should get** it.
Third conditional	**Past perfect tense**	**Modal +** *have* **+ past participle of main verb**
	If she **had asked** me earlier,	I **could have** helped her.

See Past participle, page 42.

 MORE INFORMATION

- The *if* clause can be introduced by expressions other than *if*: *as long as, provided that, so long as, unless, when, whenever.*

  Provided that I eat healthy meals, I will live a long life.

- In sentences with *were* (second conditional) or *had* (third conditional) in the *if* clause, *if* can sometimes be omitted. In this case, the verb and the subject are reversed:

  Were I in your position, I'd accept the offer. (= *If I were in your position*)

  Had I known, I would have spoken to him. (= *If I had known*)

Questions

Are you here on vacation? *Yes, I am.*
Where do you live? *I live in Sherbrooke.*
You are a student, **aren't you?** *Yes, I am.*

There are three different forms of questions in English:
- *Yes / No* questions
- Information questions
- Tag questions

8.1 *Yes / No* Questions

Is he a student? *Yes, he is. / No, he isn't.*

When do you use *yes/no* questions?

Use *yes / no* questions when the answer you are looking for is a short statement starting with *yes* or *no*.

How do you form *yes/no* questions?

Here are the ways to form *yes / no* questions.

1 When the main verb or the auxiliary verb is *be*:

See Simple Tenses, page 20.

She **is** on vacation.
They **are** going to visit Paris.
Verb *be* + subject + complement

Verb *be*	Subject	Complement	Short answer
Is	he / she	on vacation?	*Yes, he is. / No, she isn't.*
Was	he / she	an artist?	*Yes, he was. / No, she wasn't.*
Are	they	going to visit Paris?	*Yes, they are. / No, they aren't.*
Are	there	many museums in Paris?	*Yes, there are. / No, there aren't.*

2 When the main verb is not *be* and there is no auxiliary verb: See Simple Tenses, page 18.

You **like** your teacher.

Auxiliary *do* + subject + main verb + complement

Auxiliary *do*	Subject	Main verb	Complement	Short answer
Do	you	like	your teacher?	*Yes I do. / No, I don't.*
Does	he / she	make	the lessons interesting?	*Yes she does. / No, he doesn't.*
Did	they	see	the Eiffel Tower?	*Yes, they did. / No, they didn't.*

3 When the sentence contains a modal auxiliary: See Modal Auxiliaries, page 52.

She **would** like more juice.

Modal auxiliary + subject + main verb + complement

Modal auxiliary	Subject	Main verb	Complement	Short answer
Would	you / he / she	like	more juice?	*Yes, I would. / No, she wouldn't.*

4 When the sentence contains the auxiliary *have* or *had* + past participle of the main verb: See Perfect Tenses, page 40.

You **have seen** the new teacher.

He **had arrived** early in the morning.

Auxiliary *have* or *had* + subject + past participle of main verb + complement

Auxiliary *have / had*	Subject	Past participle of main verb	Complement	Short answer
Have	you	seen	the new teacher?	*Yes, I have. / No, I haven't.*
Has	he / she	taught	your class yet?	*Yes, he has. / No, she hasn't.*
Had	he / she	arrived	early in the morning?	*Yes, he had. / No, she hadn't.*

5 When the sentence contains the auxiliary *have* or *had* + *been* + present participle of the main verb:

The students **have been studying** English grammar.
They **had been expecting** a new teacher.

See Perfect Tenses, page 46.

Auxiliary *have / had* + subject + *been* + present participle of main verb + complement

Auxiliary have / had	Subject	Been + present participle of main verb	Complement	Short answer
Have	they	been studying	English grammar?	*Yes, they have. / No, they haven't.*
Had	they	been expecting	a new teacher?	*Yes, they had. / No, they hadn't.*

8.2 Information Questions

Who is Sylvia? *She is my cousin.*

When do you use information questions?

Use information questions to ask for specific information. Information questions start with a question word.

Here is a list of the most common question words.

Question word	Use it to ask about	Example	Answer
What	General information	**What** is your name?	*My name is Victoria.*
When	Time or a moment	**When** do we leave?	*We leave in five minutes.*
Where	Location, place or position	**Where** is the library?	*The library is opposite the police station.*
Who	Person or people (subject) Person or people (object, informal)	**Who** is that man over there? **Who** did you visit?	*That man is the new principal. I visited my grandparents.*
Whom	Person or people (object, formal)	**Whom** did you visit?	*I visited Mr. Richards.*
Which	Choice between items	**Which** T-shirt do you like best?	*I like the red one best.*

→

Question word	Use it to ask about	Example	Answer
Whose	Possession or relationship	**Whose** car is this?	*This is my father's car.*
Why	Reason	**Why** are you crying?	*I'm crying because I'm sad.*
How	Manner, condition or quality	**How** will you get to the station?	*I will take a taxi.*
How far	Distance	**How far** is your house?	*My house is two blocks from here.*
How long	Length or duration	**How long** was your vacation?	*My vacation was two weeks long.*
How many	Quantity that is countable	**How many** books have you read this summer?	*I have read fifteen books this summer.*
How much	Quantity that is uncountable	**How much** money have you made this summer?	*I have made $500 this summer.*
How often	Frequency	**How often** do you play hockey?	*I play hockey twice a week.*

MORE INFORMATION

Questions beginning with the question words *what, when, where, which, who, whom, whose* and *why* are often referred to as *wh* questions.

How do you form information questions?

Here are the ways to form information questions.

1 When the question word *who* is the subject of the sentence:

A man is at the door.
Nick chose this movie.

Question word + verb + complement

Question word *Who* (subject)	Verb	Complement
Who	is	at the door?
Who	chose	this movie?

2 When the main verb or the auxiliary verb is *be*: See Simple Tenses, page 20.

My book **is** in my bedroom.
The students **are** standing outside.

Question word + verb + subject + complement

Question word	Verb *be*	Subject	Complement
Where	is	my book?	
Why	are	the students	standing outside?

3 When there is no auxiliary verb and the main verb is not *be*: See Simple Tenses, page 18.

You **like** tomato ketchup on your hamburgers.

Question word + verb *do* + subject + main verb + complement

Question word	Verb *do*	Subject	Main verb	Complement
What	do	you	like	on your hamburgers?
What	did	you	do	last night?
Where	does	he	go	after school?

4 When the sentence contains a modal auxiliary: See Modal Auxiliaries, page 51.

You **should** eat fruit and vegetables to stay healthy.

Question word + modal auxiliary + subject + main verb + complement

Question word	Modal auxiliary	Subject	Main verb	Complement
What	should	you	eat	to stay healthy?
What	can	I	do	to help?
Where	will	she	buy	her fruit and vegetables?

5 When the sentence contains the auxiliary *have* or *had* + past participle of the main verb:

You **have been** somewhere all day. See Perfect Tenses, page 40.
Leon **had gone** home.

Question word + auxiliary *have* or *had* + subject + past participle of main verb + complement

Question word	Auxiliary *have* or *had*	Subject	Past participle of main verb	Complement
Where	have	you	been	all day?
Why	had	Leon	gone	home?

6 When the sentence contains the auxiliary *have* or *had* + been + present participle of the main verb + complement:

The students **have been studying** English grammar all week. See Perfect Tenses, page 46.
They **had been expecting** a new teacher.

Question word + auxiliary *have* or *had* + subject + *been* + present participle of main verb + complement

Question word	Auxiliary *have/had*	Subject	*Been* + present participle of main verb	Complement
What	have	the students	been studying	all week?
Why	had	they	been expecting	a new teacher?

⚠ **BE CAREFUL!**

Only the auxiliary verb needs to be conjugated. Make sure the auxiliary verb agrees with the subject.

Incorrect: Where ~~do he live~~?   Correct: Where **does he live**?

8.3 Tag Questions

This is fun, **isn't it?**

When do you use a tag question?

A tag question is a short question following a statement. Use tag questions to ask for confirmation of the statement.

How do you form a tag question?

1 Form a tag question using the auxiliary verb and a pronoun from the statement.
It's hot in here, **isn't it?**

2 If the statement does not contain an auxiliary, use *do*.
Claire likes ice cream, **doesn't she?**

3 Conjugate the auxiliary verb in the same tense as the previous statement.
It **was** in June, **wasn't it?**
Kevin **fell** off his bike, **didn't he?**

4 When the statement is positive, the tag is negative. When the statement is negative, the tag is positive.

Positive statement	Negative tag
You **will** (you'll) call me,	**won't** you?
You **have** (You've) lived in this house a long time,	**haven't** you?

Negative statement	Positive tag
You **are not** (aren't) leaving,	**are** you?
This **is not** (isn't) the end of the movie,	**is** it?
She **did not** (didn't) see the movie,	**did** she?

 BE CAREFUL!

Incorrect: Lauren goes to soccer practice every Monday, doesn't ~~Lauren~~?

Lauren goes to soccer practice every Monday, ~~does not~~ she?

Correct: Lauren goes to soccer practice every Monday**,** **doesn't she?**

• Use a pronoun, never a noun, as the subject in a tag question.

• Use the contracted form of the verb *be* or of the auxiliary verb to form the tag question.

• Put a comma at the end of the statement to separate it from the tag question.

Pronouns

I packed **my** luggage **myself.**
He cleaned **his** room **himself.**

Pronouns are words that replace nouns or other pronouns. ⟶ 🔼 See Nouns, page 9.

This chart shows the different types of pronouns.

	Person	Personal pronouns		Possessive adjectives and pronouns		Reflexive pronouns
		Subject	Object	Possessive adjectives	Possessive pronouns	
Singular	First	I	me	my	mine	myself
	Second	you	you	your	yours	yourself
	Third	he	him	his	his	himself
		she	her	her	hers	herself
		it	it	its	its	itself
Plural	First	we	us	our	ours	ourselves
	Second	you	you	your	yours	yourselves
	Third	they	them	their	theirs	themselves

9.1 Personal Pronouns

We bought a gift for **them**.

What are personal pronouns?

Personal pronouns take the role of subject or object in a sentence.

subject   object
She always smiles at **you**!

When do you use subject pronouns?

A subject pronoun replaces a common or a proper noun and is the subject of the verb in the sentence.

Where is **the newspaper**? **It** is on the table.
Marc and Nathalie are in love. **They** will get married next fall.

BE CAREFUL!

The first-person singular pronoun *I* is always capitalized, even when it's not the first word in a sentence.

Can **I** help you?

MORE INFORMATION

Use *he* or *she* and not *it* when referring to a pet or other animal that you know.

Be careful of that dog. **It** looks aggressive.
I like Jamie's dog. **She**'s very friendly.

When do you use object pronouns?

An object pronoun replaces the direct or indirect object of a verb or the object of a preposition.

He likes **her**.
Please send **me** your address.
He brought a gift for **me**.
The flowers are from **him**.

9.2 Possessive Adjectives and Possessive Pronouns

Her computer is much faster than **mine**.

What are possessive adjectives and possessive pronouns?

Possessive adjectives and possessive pronouns are used to indicate ownership.

Person		Possessive adjectives and pronouns	
		Possessive adjectives	Possessive pronouns
Singular	First	my	mine
	Second	your	yours
	Third	his	his
		her	hers
		its	its
Plural	First	our	ours
	Second	your	yours
	Third	their	theirs

When do you use possessive adjectives and possessive pronouns?

A possessive **adjective** indicates who owns something. Place it before the noun.

That is **my** money! Where did you put **your** money?

A possessive **pronoun** replaces a noun and its possessive adjective to show possession or ownership.

I like **my** dog better than **yours**.
(*My* is a possessive adjective. *Yours* is a possessive pronoun replacing *your dog*.)

This is not **your** book. This one is **mine**.
(*Your* is a possessive adjective. *Mine* is a possessive pronoun replacing *my book*.)

9.3 Reflexive Pronouns

I did it **myself.**

What are reflexive pronouns?

A reflexive pronoun refers to the person who does an action. It ends in *self* in the singular form or *selves* in the plural form.

Person		Reflexive pronouns
Singular	First	myself
	Second	yourself
	Third	himself
		herself
		itself
Plural	First	ourselves
	Second	yourselves
	Third	themselves

When do you use reflexive pronouns?

Use reflexive pronouns for the following situations:

1 To indicate that the subject and the object are the same

I can see **myself** in that mirror.
Can **you** see **yourself**?
She likes to study by **herself**.

2 To indicate that the subject and the indirect object are the same

He gave **himself** a birthday present.

3 To emphasize the subject

We want to solve the problem **ourselves**.

BE CAREFUL!

Pay attention to the third-personal singular and plural forms.

Incorrect: He works by ~~hisself~~.   Correct: He works by **himself**.

Incorrect: They work by ~~theirselves~~.   Correct: They work by **themselves**.

Unit 10

Indefinite and Relative Pronouns

Something that someone said made **everything** seem more interesting.

10.1 Indefinite Pronouns

Everyone loves ice cream.

What are indefinite pronouns?

Indefinite pronouns refer to unspecified people or things in the singular or plural form. They can express the idea of all, any, some or none.

When do you use indefinite pronouns?

This chart shows how to use indefinite pronouns correctly.

	Indefinite pronouns	Examples
People (singular)	anybody / anyone everybody / everyone nobody / no one somebody / someone	**Everyone** is capable of learning a new language. **Nobody** knows **anybody** who can help. **Someone** left a message.
Things (singular)	anything everything nothing something	**Anything** is possible. I've tried **everything**, but **nothing** helps. He saw **something** happening across the street.
People or things (singular)	another each either neither one	He gave **each** of them a gift. **One** cannot succeed without effort. I offered the cakes to Jon and Ella, but **neither** wanted **one**.

	Indefinite pronouns		Examples
People or things (plural)	both few many	others several	**Both** are good players, but we have **others** to consider, too. **Many** think you are a sore loser.
People or things (singular or plural)	all any more most	none some such	**All** of the pie was burnt. **All** of the hockey players are from Canada. **Most** (of the apple) **is** rotten. **Most** (of the apples) **are** ripe.

The words *all, any, more, most, none, some* and *such* are considered singular or plural depending on what they refer to.

All and *Most* in the first examples refer to one pie and one apple in the singular. They answer the question *How much?*

All and *Most* in the second examples refer to hockey players and apples in the plural. They answer the question *How many?*

 MORE INFORMATION

When referring to plural nouns, the indefinite pronoun *none* is used in the plural form only in informal language. In formal language, it is singular.

None of my friends **are** going to the party. (plural—informal)
None of the applicants **is** suitable for the job. (singular—formal)

Subject-verb agreement

When the indefinite pronoun is the subject of the sentence, always use the third-person form of the verb. If it is singular, use the third-person singular form. If it is plural, use the third-person plural form.

Everyone is going on the trip.
All of my friends **like** listening to music.
Some of the artwork **is** amazing.

Some and *any*

Indefinite pronouns that begin with *some* are used in affirmative and interrogative sentences.

Someone has taken that job.
They have **someone** for that job.
Do they have **someone** for that job?

Indefinite pronouns that begin with *any* are used in affirmative, negative and interrogative sentences.

Anyone can apply for the job.
I can't see **anyone**.
Can you see **anyone**?

 BE CAREFUL!

Indefinite pronouns *neither, no one, nobody, none* and *nothing* are already negative in meaning, so they don't need the negative form of the verb. If the verb is negative, use *either, anyone, anybody* and *anything*.

Incorrect: I ~~don't have nothing~~ to say.

Correct: I **have nothing** to say.   OR   Correct: I **don't have anything** to say.

Possessive form

To form the possessive of an indefinite pronoun that refers to a person, add **'s**.

Someone's car is parked in front of my house. ⟶ ↑ See Nouns, page 12.

|10.2| Relative Pronouns

I am reading a book **that** you recommended.

What is a relative pronoun?

A relative pronoun introduces a clause that adds information about a noun or pronoun.

When do you use relative pronouns?

This chart shows how to use relative pronouns correctly.

Pronouns	Usage	Examples
that	To add essential information	I saw the movie **that** you loved so much.
who whoever	For people (subject)	The woman **who** sang at the party was my aunt. Talk to one of the teachers, **whoever** is available. →

Indefinite and Relative Pronouns

Pronouns	Usage	Examples
whom whomever	For people (object)	The woman **whom** you saw was the English teacher. The man with **whom** I sat on the train was very pleasant. You can talk to **whomever** you please!
which whichever	To add non-essential information	The jewellery, **which** my mother gave me, was stolen. We can stay in or go out, **whichever** you prefer.
whose	To show ownership	The child **whose** parents were on television has been found!

MORE INFORMATION

In informal writing or speaking, we can use the following:

- *Who* or *that* to refer to people
  I met the artist **that** created this painting. (informal)
  I met the artist **who** created this painting. (formal and informal)

- *Who* instead of *whom* (and *whoever* instead of *whomever*) for the object of a verb.
  The teacher **who** I wanted to see was sick. (informal)
  The teacher **whom** I wanted to see was sick. (formal)

- *Who* instead of *whom* (and *whoever* instead of *whomever*) for the object of a preposition. In this case, put the preposition at the end of the "who" clause.
  The man **who** I sat on the train **with** was quite nice. (informal)
  The man **with whom** I sat on the train was very pleasant. (formal)

BE CAREFUL!

Do not confuse the relative pronoun **whose** with the contraction **who's** (*who is*).

Whose book is this?
Who's at the door?

Unit 11

Adjectives

She put on her **bright yellow** rain boots.
Her feet are **bigger than** mine.
These are my boots. **Those** boots are hers.
Her boots are **the same** colour **as** mine.

11.1 Basic Adjectives

I have a **shiny new** bike.

What are adjectives?

Adjectives give additional information about nouns and pronouns. ↑ See Nouns, page 9 and Pronouns, page 65.
They can describe, identify or quantify people, places or things.

See Nouns, page 9 and Pronouns, page 65.

How do you use adjectives?

Adjectives do not agree with the noun they are describing. They always remain the same.

a **young** girl   two **young** girls

Placing adjectives

1. An adjective usually precedes the noun it modifies.
   The **cute** dog licked my hand.

2. You can also place adjectives after the verb *be* and after non-action verbs such as *feel, look, sound.*
   The dog is **cute**.   You sound **happy**.

See Present Progressive Tense, page 35, for a list of non-action verbs.

Adjective order

If there is more than one adjective modifying a noun, they are placed in this order.

1. Opinion	2. Size	3. Age	4. Shape	5. Colour	6. Origin (nationality)	7. Material	8. Purpose
beautiful	big	new	round	red	Italian	plastic	rocking

I love this **beautiful big new round red Italian plastic rocking** chair!

Note that it is not usual to modify a noun with more than three adjectives.

Adjectives ending in *ing* and *ed*

Adjectives ending in *ing* (present participle adjectives) have an active meaning. The noun described is doing something.

See Present participle, page 34.

a **winning** team
a **talking** dog
an **exciting** movie
an **interesting** class

Adjectives ending in *ed* (past participle adjectives) have a passive meaning. The noun described is the object of the action.

See Past participle, page 42.

a **smashed** headlight
a **surprised** face
She is **excited**.
He is **interested** in art.

11.2 Comparatives and Superlatives

She is **more competent than** I am.

He is **the most romantic** guy I have ever met!

What are comparative and superlative adjectives?

Comparative adjectives are used to compare two nouns or pronouns. They indicate that someone or something has more or less of a quality than another person or thing.

Superlative adjectives compare three or more nouns or pronouns. Superlative adjectives indicate that someone or something has the most or the least of a quality.

How do you form comparative and superlative adjectives?

1 Follow these rules for most adjectives:

Form the comparative by adding **er** to the end of the adjective + **than**.

Form the superlative by adding **est** to the end of the adjective and **the** before it.

Adjective	Comparative form	Superlative form
old	old**er** than	the old**est**
tall	tall**er** than	the tall**est**

I am **the tallest** in my class because I am **older than** the other students.

2 If an adjective ends in *e*, simply add **r** to form the comparative, or **st** to form the superlative.

Adjective	Comparative form	Superlative form
large	large**r** **than**	**the** large**st**
wise	wise**r** **than**	**the** wise**st**

3 If the adjective has only one syllable and ends in a vowel and a consonant, **double the final consonant** before adding **er** or **est**.

Adjective	Comparative form	Superlative form
big	big**ger** **than**	**the** big**gest**
thin	thin**ner** **than**	**the** thin**nest**

4 With two-syllable adjectives ending in *y*, change the *y* to an *i*, then add **er** to form the comparative, or **est** to form the superlative.

Adjective	Comparative form	Superlative form
easy	eas**ier** **than**	**the** eas**iest**
happy	happ**ier** **than**	**the** happ**iest**

5 With two-syllable adjectives that end in *er, est, le, or* or *ow*, add **er** and **est**.

Adjective	Comparative form	Superlative form
narrow	narrow**er** **than**	**the** narrow**est**
simple	simpl**er** **than**	**the** simpl**est**

6 With other adjectives of two or more syllables, add *more* before the adjective to form the comparative, and *most* to form the superlative.

Adjective	Comparative form	Superlative form
modern	**more** modern **than**	**the most** modern
peaceful	**more** peaceful **than**	**the most** peaceful

7 These words can follow either the *er/est* rules above or the *more/most* rules.

Adjective	Comparative form	Superlative form
clever	clever**er than** **more** clever **than**	**the** clever**est** **the most** clever
friendly	friendl**ier than** **more** friendly **than**	**the** friendl**iest** **the most** friendly
gentle	gentl**er than** **more** gentle **than**	**the** gentl**est** **the most** gentle
quiet	quiet**er than** **more** quiet **than**	**the** quiet**est** **the most** quiet
simple	simpl**er than** **more** simple **than**	**the** simpl**est** **the most** simple

Irregular adjectives

These adjectives have special forms in the comparative and superlative.

Exceptions	Comparative form	Superlative form
bad	worse **than**	**the** worst
far	farther/further **than**	**the** farthest/furthest
good	better **than**	**the** best
little	less **than**	**the** least
many	more **than**	**the** most

? MORE INFORMATION

It is not always necessary to include *than* and the noun being compared, if it has already been mentioned:

My room is **smaller than** my sister's, but it's **quieter**.

11.3 Inferiority, Similarity and Equality

> My grade was **not as high as** Jayden's.
>
> Kassy received **the same** grade **as** I did.

How do you express inferiority, similarity and equality?

To show that something is inferior, use **less** and **the least** before the adjective.

She's **less friendly than** her brother.
She's **the least friendly** person I've ever met.

For negative comparison, you can also use the construction **not as ... as**.

She's **not as friendly as** her brother.

Express similarity or equality in the following ways:

1. Use **as (adjective) as** or **as much / many (noun) as**.
   The suede sofa is **as comfortable as** the leather sofa.
   She makes **as much money as** he does.
   I have **as many votes as** you do!

2. Use **the same (noun) as** or **the same as** for things or people that share identical traits.
   Her car is **the same colour as** mine.
   His bike is **the same as** mine.

11.4 Demonstrative Adjectives and Pronouns

> **This pen** writes well. **This** is my pen.
>
> Can I borrow **that book** you read? **That** is the book you recommended to me.

What are demonstrative adjectives and pronouns?

This, *that*, *these* and *those* can be demonstrative adjectives or demonstrative pronouns.
Demonstrative adjectives precede a noun and point to a specific person or thing.
This pen writes well.
Demonstrative pronouns identify and substitute for a noun or pronoun.
This is my pen.

How do you use demonstrative adjectives?

This / These	That / Those
This and *these* refer to nouns that are **near** in time or space.	*That* and *those* refer to nouns that are **far** in time or space.
This book here is mine. (singular) **These** bags are heavy. (plural) I don't see him often **these** days. (plural)	**That** man over there is my father. (singular) **Those** apples are too far to reach. (plural) I enjoyed **those** vacations by the lake when I was younger. (plural)

  BE CAREFUL!

This and *that* can modify the nouns *kind, sort* and *type*. When you use *these* and *those*, remember to use the plural form.

Incorrect: **these kind** of shoes   Correct: **these kinds** of shoes

Incorrect: **those sort** of movies   Correct: **those sorts** of movies

Incorrect: **these type** of people   Correct: **these types** of people

How do you use demonstrative pronouns?

This / These	That / Those
This and *these* refer to nouns or pronouns that are **near** in time or space.	*That* and *those* refer to nouns that are **far** in time or space.
This is my brother. (singular) (He is standing beside the speaker.)	**That** is my dictionary over there. (singular) (The dictionary is far from the speaker.)
These are my friends. (plural) (They are standing near the speaker.)	**Those** are your books on that table. (plural) (The books are far from the speaker.)
This is the happiest day of my life. (singular) (The day is today.)	**That** was a terrible day. (singular) (The day is in the past.)

Adverbs

We **often** visit my grandparents.

My mother drives **more slowly than** my father.

My brother plays hockey **less often than** I do.

He plays **as well as** I do.

An adverb modifies a verb, an adjective or even another adverb. An adverb tells you how, where or when something is done.

12.1 Types of Adverbs

I called her **yesterday**.

Richard walks **slowly**.

What are the different types of adverbs?

Here are the different types of adverbs.

1 **Adverbs of frequency and time**

These answer the questions *When?* (time) and *How often?* (frequency)

Common adverbs of frequency include these:

always   frequently   never   occasionally   often   rarely   usually

Common adverbs of time include these:

already   eventually   finally   lately   now   recently   soon   today   tomorrow   yesterday

Place an adverb of frequency and time before the main verb.

She **often** travels to Vancouver.   We **finally** saw the movie.

If the main verb is *be* and there is no auxiliary, place the adverb of frequency or time after the verb *be*.

They are **always** home when we call.

If there is an auxiliary, the adverb goes before the main verb (*be*) as usual.

We will **soon** be at their house.

❋ **EXCEPTIONS**

The adverbs of time *today*, *tomorrow*, *tonight* and *yesterday* are placed at the end of the sentence.

They are home **today**.
We went to their house **yesterday**.

---

2 Adverbs of manner

This is the largest group of adverbs. They answer the question *How?*
Most adverbs of manner end in *ly*.

Here are a few examples of adverbs of manner:

badly   carefully   dangerously   happily   quickly   simply   terribly

Follow these rules for placing adverbs of manner in a sentence:

a) Place an adverb of manner after a verb but before an adjective or adverb.
    Anthony drove **carefully**.
    Chloe is **happily** married.
    The car thief drove **dangerously** fast.

b) If there is a direct object, place the adverb after the object.
    Anthony drove <u>his new car</u> **carefully**.

See Sentence Structure, page 99.

c) If the direct object is long, place the adverb before the verb.
    Anthony **carefully** drove <u>his brand new red sports car</u>.

3 Adverbs of place and distance

These answer the question *Where?*

Common adverbs of place and distance include these:

above   below   far   nearby   here   there   inside   outside   upstairs   downstairs

Put an adverb of place and distance after the direct object or the verb.
She walked **upstairs**.
She took <u>her presents</u> **upstairs**.

When there is a long complement to the verb, you can place the adverb at the beginning of the sentence.

Upstairs, you will find <u>everything you need ready for you</u>.

4 Adverbs of degree and intensity

These answer the questions *How much?* or *How little?* They help us understand the strength or intensity of something.

Common adverbs of degree and intensity include these:

almost   extremely   really   so   too   very

Place an adverb of degree and intensity before the adjective, adverb or verb it modifies.

The pool was **very** cold.

He has **almost** finished his homework.

EXCEPTIONS

The adverb *enough* follows the adjective it modifies.

My passport photo isn't very good, but it's **good enough**.

How do you form adverbs?

Many adverbs end with the suffix *ly*. You can create these adverbs by adding the suffix **ly** to the end of an adjective.

slow → slow**ly**   quick → quick**ly**

See Adjectives, page 73 and Phrasal Verbs and Other Words, page 117.

Spelling Rules

Follow these rules to form adverbs.

Rules	Examples
Add **ly** to the end of an adjective.	quiet → quiet**ly**
If an adjective already ends in *y*, change the *y* to *i* and add **ly**.	happy → happ**ily**
If the adjective ends in *le*, change the final *e* to **y**.	terrible → terrib**ly**
If the adjective ends in *ic*, add **ally**.	basic → basic**ally**
For the adjectives *true*, *due* and *whole*, drop the final *e* before adding **ly**.	true → tru**ly** due → du**ly** whole → who**lly**

Some adverbs are irregular. Here are some examples.

Adjectives	Irregular adverbs
early	early
far	far
fast	fast
good	well
hard	hard
high	high
late	late

Some adverbs do not end in *ly* and do not have an equivalent adjective, including these:

already   now   soon   today   tomorrow   yesterday   yet

BE CAREFUL!

Some adjectives already end in *ly* and cannot be changed into adverbs, for example, *friendly, lonely, silly, ugly*. The meaning then has to be expressed differently, for example:

He's very **friendly**.
He talks **in a friendly way**.

An exception is *early*. This can be used as an adjective and adverb.

12.2 Comparative and Superlative Adverbs

Chris drives **more carefully than** Alexis.

Max drives **the most carefully** of them all.

What are comparative and superlative adverbs?

Use comparative and superlative adverbs to compare verbs, adjectives and other adverbs.

Comparative adverbs describe the difference between two verbs, adjectives or adverbs.

Superlative adverbs compare three or more verbs, adjectives or adverbs.

How do you form comparative and superlative adverbs?

1 If the adverb ends in *ly*, add ***more*** before the adverb to form the comparative, and ***the most*** to form the superlative.

Adjective	Adverb	Comparative adverb	Superlative adverb
quiet	quietly	**more** quietly **than**	**the most** quietly

2 If the adverb does not end in *ly* or is the same as its adjective form, add ***er*** for the comparative and ***est*** for the superlative. ⟶ ⬆ See Adjectives, page 74 for the comparative and superlative forms.

Adjective	Adverb	Comparative adverb	Superlative adverb
fast	fast	fast**er than**	**the** fast**est**
early	early	earl**ier than**	**the** earl**iest**
hard	hard	hard**er than**	**the** hard**est**
high	high	high**er than**	**the** high**est**
late	late	lat**er than**	**the** lat**est**

3 These adverbs are irregular in the comparative and superlative.

Adjective	Adverb	Comparative adverb	Superlative adverb
far	far	farther / further	farthest / furthest
good	well	better	best
bad	badly	worse	worst

12.3 Inferiority, Similarity and Equality

> Iris writes **less clearly than** Rose.
>
> Iris sings **as beautifully as** her mother.

To show that something is inferior, use the expressions ***less (adverb) than*** and ***the least (adverb)***.

Alexis drives **less carefully than** Chris.
He drives **the least carefully** of everyone I know.

You can also use the construction ***not as (adverb) as***.

Alexis does **not** drive **as carefully as** Chris.

Use the expression ***as (adverb) as*** to express similarity or equality.

Jack speaks **as fluently as** Mary.   Liam plays the guitar **as well as** Lily.
Sara tells jokes **as funnily as** Noah.

Infinitives and Gerunds

Julia likes **to travel**.

I enjoy **swimming** in lakes.

13.1 Infinitives

I plan **to travel** around the world.

What are infinitives?

Infinitives are verbs that can be used as nouns. They can be the subject or complement of a verb.

To travel is important in life. (subject)   Julia likes **to travel**. (complement)

Infinitives are formed with *to* + the base form of the verb.

to + be = to be

How do you use infinitives?

Some verbs are followed by an infinitive. Here is a list of the most common verbs that are followed by an infinitive:

afford	claim	fail	need	promise
agree	decide	hope	offer	refuse
appear	demand	learn	plan	seem
arrange	deserve	manage	prepare	wait
ask	expect	mean	pretend	want

I **intend to study** this morning.   She **wants to dance** all night.

13.2 Gerunds

Swimming is good for you.

What are gerunds?

Gerunds are verbs ending in *ing* that are used as nouns. They can be the subject or the complement of a verb or the object of a preposition.

Cycling is fun. (subject)
I enjoy **kayaking**. (complement)
After swimming, I am always hungry. (object of a preposition)

Gerunds are formed with the base form of the verb + ***ing***.

play + *ing* = playing See Progressive Verbs, page 34, for spelling rules for the *ing* ending.

How do you use gerunds?

Here is a list of the most common verbs that are followed by a gerund, not an infinitive:

admit	complete	finish	practise	resent
advise	consider	keep	quit	resist
anticipate	deny	mention	recall	risk
appreciate	dislike	mind	recommend	suggest
avoid	enjoy	miss	regret	understand

Tanja **keeps talking** about her dog.   I **understand** your **wanting** to leave.
They **enjoy listening** to music.

Gerund after the verb *go*

The verb *go* is often followed by a gerund to express doing recreational activities or adventure sports. Here are some examples:

Recreational activities	Adventure sports
go bowling	go jogging
go bungee jumping	go kayaking
go climbing	go running
go dancing	go shopping
go hiking	go snorkling
go hunting	go skateboarding

Did she **go hiking** last weekend?   We **went jogging** last night.

BE CAREFUL!

Don't confuse a gerund with the progressive tense.

Right now, I **am swimming** in the lake. (present progressive tense)
I enjoy **swimming** in the lake. (gerund)

Infinitive or Gerund?

Remember **to mail** the letter.

I remember **mailing** it yesterday.

Some verbs can be followed by either an infinitive or a gerund. Be careful, because using the infinitive or gerund can change the meaning of these verbs.

Verbs with the same meanings

Here are some common verbs that can be followed by both gerunds and infinitives and have the same or almost the same meaning:

Verb	Example with gerund	Example with infinitive
begin	It began **snowing**.	It began **to snow**.
continue	He continued **running**.	He continued **to run**.
hate	She hates **shopping**.	She hates **to shop**.
intend	I intend **going** to the concert.	I intend **to go** to the concert.
like	We like **seeing** movies.	We like **to see** movies.
love	They love **fishing**.	They love **to fish**.
prefer	We prefer **hiking**.	We prefer **to hike**.
start	Max has started **exercising**.	Max has started **to exercise**.

Verbs with different meanings

Here are some common verbs that can be followed by both gerunds and infinitives but have different meanings:

Verb	Examples	Meanings
forget	She forgot **to book** the room. She never forgot **feeling** hungry all the time.	forget + **infinitive** = forget to do a task forget + **gerund** = forget something from the past

Verb	Examples	Meanings
remember	Luna remembers **to sit** when told. I remember **seeing** you last week.	remember + **infinitive** = remember to do a task remember + **gerund** = remember something from the past
stop	He stopped **to talk** to his teacher. He stopped **talking** when I arrived.	stop + **infinitive** = purpose, stop in order to do something stop + **gerund** = stop an activity in progress
try	I tried **to learn** Arabic. I tried **telling** you, but it didn't change anything.	try + **infinitive** = effort try + **gerund** = experiment

Passive Voice

The package **was sent** yesterday.

What is the passive voice?

In the active voice, the subject is doing the action.

subject	verb	direct object
Victoria	**threw**	the ball.

In the passive voice, the subject is not doing the action. The subject is *passive*. The agent is the person or thing doing the action.

subject	verb	agent
The ball	**was thrown**	by Victoria.

When do you use the passive voice?

Use the passive voice in the following situations:

1. When the agent of the action is unknown or unimportant
   My house **has been robbed**. (By whom is unknown.)

2. When the agent of the action is obvious, so we don't have to state it
   Sabrina's homework **was handed in** on time.

3. When you want to draw attention to the agent of the action
   The man was struck **by lightning**.
   The story was written **by Edgar Allan Poe**.

We use the passive voice most often in situation 1 above. It is best to use mainly the active voice in your writing.

How do you form a passive sentence?

You can form a passive sentence by looking at an active sentence.

1. Make the direct object the subject of the passive sentence.
2. Identify the verb tense of the active verb.
3. Conjugate *be* in the same tense as the active verb.
4. Add the past participle of the active verb. ─── See Past participle, page 42, and the Irregular Verbs Chart, page 125.

Active sentence

subject	verb	direct object
Her father	**pays**	the rent. (simple present)

Passive sentence

subject	simple present tense of *be*	past participle	agent
The rent	**is**	**paid**	by her father.

You can form a passive sentence in any verb tense. Here are the most common tenses.

Tense	Active voice	Passive voice
Simple present *am / are / is* + past participle	His reaction surprises me.	I **am surprised** by his reaction.
Simple past *was / were* + past participle	His reaction surprised me.	I **was surprised** by his reaction.
Simple future *will be* + past participle	They will sign the contract tomorrow.	The contract **will be signed** tomorrow.
Present progressive *am / are / is being* + past participle	The tutors are helping students.	Students **are being helped** by tutors.
Past progressive *was / were being* + past participle	The guests were eating the pancakes.	The pancakes **were being eaten** by the guests.
Present perfect *have / has been* + past participle	Ice storms have destroyed many trees.	Many trees **have been destroyed** by ice storms.
Present / Future tense with modal auxiliary modal + *be* + past participle	They should sign the contract today / tomorrow.	The contract **should be signed** today / tomorrow.
Past tense with modal auxiliary modal + *have been* + past participle	They could have signed the contract yesterday.	The contract **could have been signed** yesterday.

The rules for forming negatives, interrogatives and tag questions remain unchanged.

Negative	Interrogative	Tag question
Simple present tense		
I **am (I'm) not surprised** by his reaction.	**Am** I **surprised** by his reaction?	I **am (I'm) surprised** by his reaction, **aren't** I?
Simple past tense		
I **was not (wasn't) surprised** by his reaction.	**Was** I **surprised** by his reaction?	I **was surprised** by his reaction, **wasn't** I?
Simple Future Tense		
The contract **will not (won't) be signed** tomorrow.	**Will** the contract **be signed** tomorrow?	The contract **will be signed** tomorrow, **won't** it?
Present progressive tense		
Students **are not (aren't) being helped** by tutors.	**Are** students **being helped** by tutors?	Students **are being helped** by tutors, **aren't** they?
Past progressive tense		
The pancakes **were not (weren't) being eaten** by the guests.	**Were** the pancakes **being eaten** by the guests?	The pancakes **were being eaten** by the guests, **weren't** they?
Present perfect tense		
Many trees **have not (haven't) been destroyed** by ice storms.	**Have** many trees **been destroyed** by ice storms?	Many trees **have been destroyed** by ice storms, **haven't** they?
Present / Future tense with modal auxiliary		
The contract **should not (shouldn't) be signed** today / tomorrow.	**Should** the contract **be signed** today / tomorrow?	The contract **should be signed** today / tomorrow, **shouldn't** it?
Past tense with modal auxiliary		
The contract **could not (couldn't) have been signed** yesterday.	**Could** the contract **have been signed** yesterday?	The contract **could have been signed** yesterday, **couldn't** it?

See page 89.

MORE INFORMATION

Only verbs that take a direct object can be used in the passive voice. Other verbs cannot be used in the passive voice, for example: *appear, belong, care, consist (of), exist, fall, go, happen, matter, occur, result (from), rise, seem.*

Reported Speech

> She said, "I'm busy!"
> **She said she was busy.**

Reported speech states what someone said without using quotation marks. The verbs used to report speech are generally *say* or *tell*.

How do you form reported speech?

Here is how to change direct speech to reported speech:

Direct speech: He said, "I am leaving next week."

1. Change the pronoun and the verb tense (see chart on page 92).
   He said **he was** leaving.

2. Change the time reference (if needed).
   He said he was leaving **the following** week.

3. After the verb *say*, it is not mandatory to use the preposition *to* and an object. It is mandatory, however, to use an object when using the verb *tell*.
   She said (to me) she was coming. (preposition and object optional)
   She told **me** she was coming. (object mandatory)

? MORE INFORMATION

Direct speech is also called quoted speech.

Reported speech is also called indirect speech.

Verb tenses

Use the simple past tense as the main verb in reported speech since you are reporting what someone said to you in the past. The chart below shows how to change the tenses in direct speech to those required for reported speech.

Direct speech	Change	Reported speech
He said, "I **am** thirsty."	Simple present → simple past	He said he **was** thirsty.
She said, "I **worked** all day yesterday."	Simple past → past perfect	She said she **had worked** all day the previous day.
He said, "I'**m leaving** on Saturday."	Present progressive → past progressive	He said he **was leaving** the following Saturday.
He said, "I **was running** earlier."	Past progressive → past perfect progressive	He said he **had been running** earlier.
She said, "I'**ve been** tired a lot lately."	Present perfect → past perfect	She said she **had been** tired a lot lately.
He said, "I'**ve been living** in this house for seven years."	Present perfect progressive → past perfect progressive	He said he **had been living** in that house for seven years.
She said, "The class **had** already **started** when he arrived."	Past perfect → past perfect (no change)	She said the class **had** already **started** when he arrived.
He said, "I **had been driving** for hours."	Past perfect progressive → past perfect progressive (no change)	He said he **had been driving** for hours.
She said, "I'**ll be** there tomorrow."	Simple future modal auxiliary will → would	She said she **would be** there tomorrow.
He said, "I **can be** there at nine."	Modal auxiliary can → could	He said he **could be** there at nine.
She said, "I **must get** at least eighty percent on the test."	Modal auxiliary must → had to	She said she **had to get** at least eighty percent on the test.

There is no change to *could, would, should, might* and *ought to.*

He said, "I **should practise** more." → He said he **should practise** more.

Common verbs for reported speech

You can use different verbs for reported speech.
Here is a list of common reporting verbs.

admit	deny	reply
agree	explain	say
ask	mention	suggest
complain	promise	tell

Direct speech	Reported speech
"I didn't prepare for the test."	He **admitted** that he hadn't prepared for the test.
"I'll call him tomorrow."	She **promised** she would call him the next day.
"I didn't tell her."	He **denied** that he had told her.
"The other team didn't play fair!"	They **complained** that the other team hadn't played fair.

Reported questions

When reporting direct questions, follow the same tense changes as shown for direct speech in the chart on page 92. Use a question verb, such as *ask*, in place of *say* and add *if* or *whether*. Use affirmative sentence structure, not question form.

Direct question	Reported question
He asked, "**Are** you thirsty?"	He asked **if I was** thirsty.
She asked, "**Does** he **like** cheese?"	She asked **whether he liked** cheese.

Prepositions

My piano classes start **at** six o'clock **on** Monday evening.

A preposition is a word that usually comes before a noun or pronoun to show time, place and direction.

How do you use prepositions?

The following charts show the different types of prepositions and how to use them correctly.

Time

These prepositions answer the question *When?* or *How long?*

Preposition	Example
at	I work **at** night. My mom started dancing **at** forty-one years old.
before	I started playing hockey **before** 2011.
by	I will be finished **by** ten o'clock.
during	I hate travelling **during** rush hour.
for	I've been doing judo **for** three years.
in	My appointment is **in** thirty minutes / **in** August / **in** winter / **in** 2014 / **in** the morning.
on	The party is **on** Saturday / **on** my birthday / **on** March 26.
since	My father has been playing guitar **since** 1972.
to / until	My class is from Monday **to** Thursday **until** next December.

Place

These prepositions answer the question *Where?*

Preposition	Example
above	She is holding the mistletoe **above** my head.
across	I will swim **across** the lake.
against	The waves are crashing **against** the rocks.
at	Simon is **at** a rock concert.
behind	Leo is hiding **behind** that tree.
below	The fish are **below** the surface.
beneath	The Titanic is **beneath** the Atlantic Ocean.
between	Please sit **between** John and Luke.
by / next to / beside	Emma is waiting **by** / **next to** / **beside** the car.
from	They are flowers **from** the garden.
in / inside	I'm **in** the living room. Your gift is **inside** that box.
into	Lucy walked **into** the kitchen.
near	My bag is **near** the door.
on	My cat is **on** the counter / **on** the right / **on** the second floor / **on** the bus / **on** a plane / **on** TV / **on** the radio.
outside	The dog is waiting **outside** the store.
over	Wear a sweater **over** your T-shirt.
to	Is Toni going **to** your house tonight?
under	The book is **under** the desk.
underneath	She is wearing a shirt **underneath** her sweater.
up / down	Can you climb **up** that tree and then climb **down** again?

Travel and movement

These prepositions answer the question *Where to / from?* or *How?*

Preposition	Example
by	She travels to school **by** bus.
in / out of	Get **in** the taxi. Get **out of** the car.
off	You have to get **off** the subway at Atwater station.
on	Get **on** the bus or else you'll be late for karate.
over	Don't climb **over** the fence!
through	Mara travels **through** a tunnel to get to school.
to	Mark, go **to** bed!
toward	If you walk **toward** the park, you'll find my house.

Other prepositions

Preposition	Example
about	The movie is **about** a space invasion.
by	This is a book **by** Margaret Atwood.
of	Silvana is a friend **of** mine.

Prepositions of time and place

These three prepositions can be used for either time or place.

Preposition	Time	Examples	Place	Examples
at	time (on a clock)	**at** ten o'clock	address area general place	**at** 1243 Main Street **at** the swimming pool **at** the rock concert
in	month season year decade historical period	**in** March **in** spring **in** 2012 **in** the 1980s **in** the Middle Ages	building (inside) city province country	**in** jail **in** Toronto **in** Alberta **in** Italy
on	date day of the week	**on** July 23 **on** Monday	street	**on** Main Street

BE CAREFUL!

Be careful not to make these common mistakes.

Incorrect	Correct
He will go ~~at~~ Ottawa on the weekend.	He will go **to** Ottawa on the weekend.
We arrived ~~to~~ the cottage yesterday.	We arrived **at** the cottage yesterday.
He accused her ~~for~~ cheating.	He accused her **of** cheating.
They are not afraid ~~from~~ dogs.	They are not afraid **of** dogs.
Miguel was angry ~~against~~ the waiter.	Miguel was angry **with** the waiter.

Sentence Structure

Joey parked his car.

He wanted to buy a book, but he had lost his wallet.

He searched for the wallet that he had lost.

A sentence is a group of words that expresses a complete idea. There are three types of sentences: **simple**, **compound** and **complex**.

17.1 Simple Sentences

Joey parked his car outside the bookstore.

What is a simple sentence?

A simple sentence contains only one independent clause and can be as short as one word.

Look!

A sentence always starts with a capital letter and ends with a period,

Joey parked his car**.**

an exclamation mark

See Basics, page 8, and Punctuation and Capitalization, page 108.

Joey drove his car into the river**!**

or a question mark.

Why did Joey drive his car into the river**?**

> **? MORE INFORMATION**
>
> In the sentence *Joey parked his car,* **his car** is the direct object of the verb **parked**.
>
> | Subject | Verb | Direct object |
> |---------|------|---------------|
> | Joey | parked | his car. |

What is a clause?

A clause contains a subject and a verb. There are two kinds of clauses: independent clauses and dependent clauses.

1 Independent clause

An independent clause expresses a complete idea and can stand by itself.
Joey wanted to buy a book.

2 Dependent clause

A dependent clause does not express a complete idea. It is part of a sentence and cannot stand by itself. A dependent clause needs an independent clause to complete it.

A dependent clause begins with either a subordinating conjunction or a relative pronoun.

... **because** it looked interesting. (subordinating conjunction) ⬇ See Conjunctions and Transitions, page 102

... **that** a friend had recommended. (relative pronoun)

⬆ See Relative Pronouns, page 71.

17.2 Compound Sentences

He wanted to buy a book, but he had lost his wallet.

What is a compound sentence?

A compound sentence contains two or more independent clauses. It joins a minimum of two complete ideas.

How do you form a compound sentence?

There are three kinds of compound sentences:

1. Clauses joined by a coordinating conjunction		
Independent clause + comma	coordinating conjunction	independent clause
Mary saw the wallet on the floor,	**and**	she picked it up.

→

2. Clauses joined by a semicolon		
Independent clause + semicolon		independent clause
Mary saw the wallet on the floor;		she picked it up.
3. Clauses joined by a semicolon and a transition word		
Independent clause + semicolon	transition word + comma	independent clause
Mary saw the wallet on the floor;	**then,**	she picked it up.

MORE INFORMATION

- The independent clause is sometimes called the main clause.
- Transition words are also called adverbial conjunctions.

17.3 Complex Sentences

Mary found the wallet that Joey had lost.

What is a complex sentence?

A complex sentence contains one independent clause and at least one dependent clause. The dependent clause can start with a subordinating conjunction or a relative pronoun.

Mary found the wallet **when** she moved the sofa. (subordinating conjunction)
Mary found the wallet **that** Joey was looking for. (relative pronoun)

How do you form complex sentences?

The dependent clause can come before or after the independent clause. When the dependent clause comes before the independent clause, the clauses are separated by a comma.

When Mary moved the sofa, she found the wallet.

When the independent clause comes before the dependent clause, the comma may be omitted.

Mary found the wallet **when** she moved the sofa.

? MORE INFORMATION

The dependent clause is also called the subordinate clause.

Types of dependent clauses

There are three types of dependent clauses: adjective clauses, adverb clauses and noun clauses.

1 An **adjective clause** is a dependent clause that modifies a noun or pronoun. It always starts with a relative pronoun such as *that, which* or *who*.

The wallet **that Mary found** is on the table.
We **who are fortunate** should help others.

Adjective clauses answer questions such as *Which? What? What kind of?* and *Who?*

2 An **adverb clause** is a dependent clause that modifies a verb, adjective or another adverb. It almost always starts with a subordinating conjunction such as *because* or *when*.

Joey parked his car **as if nothing was wrong**.
Mary was surprised **when she found the wallet**.
Joey drove home immediately, **because he was worried**.

Adverb clauses answer the questions *Why? Where? When? How? To what extent?* and *Under what condition?*

3 A **noun clause** is a clause which takes the place of a noun.

What Joey discovered shocked him.
Joey's wallet is **what is missing**.
Joey hopes to discover **who has his wallet**.
Mary knows **where it is**.

Noun clauses answer the questions *Who?* and *What?*

Conjunctions and Transitions

Alex **and** Tina wrote a book.

In addition, they worked with Jon.

18.1 Conjunctions

This pizza is hot **and** delicious.

What are conjunctions?

Conjunctions are words that connect words, phrases and clauses. There are three kinds of conjunctions:

1 Coordinating conjunctions
2 Subordinating conjunctions
3 Paired conjunctions

How do you use conjunctions?

Here is how to use these different kinds of conjunctions.

Coordinating conjunctions

A coordinating conjunction connects the following:

1 Words that have the same function, for example, two nouns, two verbs, two adjectives

   My sister wants a doll **and** a truck for her birthday.
   We can choose hiking **or** swimming for our afternoon activity.
   I find her intelligent **but** unfriendly.

2 Two independent clauses in a compound sentence See Sentence Structure, page 99.

I can lend you the money, **but** you must pay me back.

The following chart lists the seven coordinating conjunctions.

Coordinating conjunction	Function	Examples
and	Introduces an addition	I'm going to bring bread **and** cheese to the party. Chris goes to school, **and** he has a part-time job.
but	Indicates contrast	He likes skiing **but** not snowboarding. I'd like to go, **but** I have to work.
for	Introduces a reason	My heart was broken, **for** she had refused my proposal.
nor	Indicates a negative alternative	She doesn't ski, **nor** does she snowboard.
or	Indicates an alternative	We can have fish **or** chicken for supper. You can go fishing, **or** you can go hiking.
so	Shows a result	He arrived late, **so** he missed the explanations.
yet	Indicates contrast	She is quiet **yet** friendly. He was nice to me, **yet** I know he doesn't like me.

MORE INFORMATION

- The conjunctions *for* and *nor* are more formal and are mainly used in writing.
- After **nor**, reverse the subject and verb.

  She doesn't ski, **and she doesn't** snowboard.

  She doesn't ski, **nor does she** snowboard.

There are three rules when using coordinating conjunctions in a compound sentence.

1 Make sure each clause of the sentence is independent. See Sentence Structure, page 99.

It was snowing heavily.   School was cancelled for the day.

2 Place the coordinating conjunctions in between the clauses.

It was snowing heavily, **so** school was cancelled for the day.

3 Use a comma before the conjunction.

It was snowing heavily**,** so school was cancelled for the day.

Subordinating conjunctions

A subordinating conjunction introduces a dependent clause in a complex sentence.

Since I prefer math, I did my math exercises first.

A subordinating conjunction can be used to introduce information that is less important in the sentence.

> ↑ See Sentence Structure, page 100.

The following chart lists the most common subordinating conjunctions.

Subordinating conjunction	Function	Examples
after before	Indicates a sequence	**After** I arrived home, I texted my friend. **Before** she went to school, she studied for the test.
although even though	Indicates contrast	**Although** he practises the violin every day, he plays poorly. She went to the party **even though** she was tired.
as just as	Indicates comparison	**As** the meteorologist had predicted, it snowed on Monday. He came first in the competition, **just as** everyone expected.
	Indicates interrupted action	**As** I was crossing the road, a car drove in front of me.
because since so that	Indicates a reason	Sam is staying home **because** he is sick. **Since** she loves animals, she is going to adopt a cat. They are taking intensive English **so that** they can become bilingual.
even if if unless	Introduces a condition	**Even if** we leave right away, we won't arrive on time. **If** you can't come today, we will go out another time. He will ride his bike to school **unless** it rains.
until	Indicates a specific time	We can swim in the lake **until** it gets dark.
when	Indicates a time	**When** they went to New York City, they visited the Empire State Building.
where wherever	Introduces a place	They don't know **where** they are going on vacation. They will go **wherever** they want to go.
whether	Introduces a choice or condition	We are going to the concert **whether** you like it or not!
while	Shows actions happening at the same time	**While** I was washing the dishes, she was reading.

Follow these rules when using subordinating conjunctions.

1 A dependent clause can come before or after an independent clause.

I'll go skiing **if I can find my skis**.

If I can find my skis, I'll go skiing.

2 If a dependent clause comes before an independent clause, the clauses are separated by a comma.

Before I go skiing, I will check the weather forecast.

3 If a dependent clause comes after an independent clause, a comma between the clauses is not usually necessary.

He will ride his bike to school unless it rains.

Paired conjunctions

A paired conjunction consists of two coordinating conjunctions used together for emphasis. The same grammatical structure follows each conjunction. They always link together equal elements, for example, two nouns, two adjectives, two verbs or two independent clauses.

 MORE INFORMATION

Paired conjunctions are also known as correlative conjunctions.

Here is a list of the most common paired conjunctions.

Paired conjunctions	Function	Examples
as ... as	Indicates equality	My cat is **as** intelligent **as** your dog.
either ... or	Indicates alternatives	I told him, it's **either** me **or** her! **Either** you stop seeing her, **or** we are finished.
both ... and	Indicates dual inclusion	**Both** my father **and** my mother will be coming for supper.
neither ... nor	Indicates dual exclusion, negation	**Neither** Lucas **nor** Mia said anything about this. Lucas **neither** spoke about the incident **nor** took any action.
not only ... but also	Indicates inclusion	He won **not only** the first prize **but also** the second prize. **Not only** did he win both prizes, **but** he **also** met the author J. K. Rowling.
whether ... or	Indicates two alternative conditions	**Whether** hot **or** cold, pizza is delicious. **Whether** you come **or** you stay at home is not a big deal.

MORE INFORMATION

- After (*neither*)... **nor** and **not only** ... (*but also*), reverse the subject and verb *be* or modal auxiliary.

  He neither likes algebra, **nor is he** good at it.

  If there is no verb *be* or modal auxiliary, use the auxiliary *do* + main verb.

  Not only did she pay back the money, but she also bought me lunch.

- When using *so*, *neither* or *nor* to agree with someone, the subject and verb must be reversed following the conjunction.

  I love playing video games. **So do I!**

  I am not good at algebra. **Neither am I! / Nor am I!**

See Modal Auxiliaries, page 51.

18.2 Transition Words and Expressions

Chloe went to Europe last summer. **Moreover**, she paid for the whole trip herself.

What are transition words?

Transition words link two complete ideas either in two separate sentences or in two independent clauses separated by a semicolon. They show the relationship between the sentences or ideas.

How do you use transition words?

Follow these rules when using transition words.

1. Check that there are two separate but linked sentences.

   The bus broke down on the way to the terminus. He was late for the exam. (The second sentence is the result of the first.)

2. Then add a transition word, followed by a comma, to the beginning of the second sentence.

   The bus broke down on the way to the terminus. **Therefore,** he was late for the exam.

3. Alternatively, join the sentences: place a semicolon at the end of the first sentence and a transition word, followed by a comma, at the beginning of the second sentence. Do not capitalize the transition word.

   The bus broke down on the way to the terminus; **therefore,** he was late for the exam.

MORE INFORMATION

Transition words are also known as adverbial conjunctions.

Use transition words in the following situations:

Transition words	Function	Examples
additionally also besides furthermore in addition in fact moreover	Add information	Remember to study for your exam. **Also**, don't forget to bring a dictionary to class. I don't need a new bike. **Besides**, I don't have the money to buy one. I like History. **In fact**, it's my favourite subject.
alternatively instead on the contrary on the other hand otherwise	Indicate an alternative	He is very strict. **On the other hand**, he is always very helpful. We must buy our tickets today; **otherwise**, they might be sold out.
despite (that) however nevertheless nonetheless	Indicate contrast	He is not tall. **Despite that**, he's an excellent basketball player. She is a vegetarian; **however**, she eats fish.
eventually finally later meanwhile next subsequently then	Indicate time	I waited for George for an hour. **Eventually**, he arrived. Emma was late as usual. **Meanwhile**, her friend made a to-do list.
for example for instance	Introduce an example	You can make a healthy lunch. **For example**, try a salad.
consequently therefore thus	Show a result	He was injured in the accident. **Therefore**, he needed medical attention.
in conclusion to conclude	Indicate a conclusion	**In conclusion**, I believe that it is important to be aware of this issue.

 BE CAREFUL!

Use a comma after a transition word or expression.

It wasn't raining. On the contrary, it was a beautiful day.
It wasn't raining; on the contrary, it was a beautiful day.

Punctuation and Capitalization

My brother—who was watching from the riverbank—suddenly shouted, "Look out!"

I'm reading *The Adventures of Huckleberry Finn* by **M**ark **T**wain in **E**nglish class.

19.1 Punctuation

He said, "That was amazing!"

What are punctuation marks?

Punctuation marks are symbols that help make sentences clear. Punctuation tells the reader how to interpret the message.

When do you use punctuation?

The following chart shows how to use different types of punctuation.

Type of punctuation	Functions	Examples
Period (.)	• At the end of a sentence • With most abbreviations • After initials	She finished supper. Mrs. Thomas is a great teacher. W. O. Mitchell is a Canadian author. →

Type of punctuation	Functions	Examples
Comma (,)	• Before a conjunction that separates independent clauses	She turned sixteen, so she registered for driving lessons.
	• Before a direct quote	She said, "It was cool!"
	• Between two numbers	He found 15, 3 more than me.
	• To separate items in a list	He bought a sweater, a pair of jeans, some socks and a pair of shoes.
	• To separate a dependent clause from an independent clause	As you can see, it's very effective.
	• Before and after non-essential information in a sentence	Joanna, who was listening, said nothing.
		Chris, the guitarist, can play five instruments.
	• Before the year in a date	December 31, 2012
	• To separate thousands and hundreds in a number	26,786
Question mark (?)	• To indicate a question	How old are you?
Exclamation mark (!)	• To indicate a strong emotion	It was amazing!
	• After a command / order	Stand up!
Semicolon (;)	• To link two independent clauses in one sentence without using a coordinating conjunction	Going on a hot-air balloon ride is not scary; it's thrilling!
	• For lists that include an item that contains a comma	It's been a busy week. On Monday, I worked at the store; on Tuesday, I babysat my neighbour's child; on Wednesday, I worked again; and on Thursday, I went to the water park with my friends.
Colon (:)	• To introduce a list of things, an explanation or a formal quotation longer than three lines	To write a text, you will need the following: a pencil, an eraser and a sheet of paper.
	• Between titles and subtitles	Curling: Techniques and Strategies
	• After a business letter salutation	Dear Mr. Douglas:
	• Between hours and minutes	It's 5:45 p.m.
Parentheses ( )	• To give clarity or more information	Michael (my brother) is very friendly.
	• To reference pages, chapters, units and so on	See Nouns (page 9).

Punctuation and Capitalization

Type of punctuation	Functions	Examples
Apostrophe (')	• To indicate possession • To indicate the contracted form of verbs	This is Ann's bicycle. I'm sorry, I've forgotten your name.
Quotation marks (" ")	• To show a direct quote • To indicate titles of newspaper and magazine articles, chapters, poems, songs, short stories, essays, TV episodes	Paul whispered, "What are we doing here?" We heard "Diamonds" by Rihanna on the radio this morning.
Single quotation marks (' ')	• To indicate a quote inside a direct quote	Trina said, "We all heard the teacher say 'no homework today,' so we're free for the weekend."
Hyphen (-)	• Used in compound numbers written as words • Used in some compound nouns • To divide a word at the end of a line by respecting the syllables • Sometimes to add a prefix to a word	My brother is twenty-one years old. My great-aunt is visiting us. Ricardo will be leaving for Colum-bia in two weeks. Erica seems anti-social. She always eats alone.
Ellipsis (…)	• To indicate that words in a quote have been omitted • To indicate an unfinished idea	The prime minister said, "We are a great nation … and we will change the world!" All I heard was, "Call the police, I …" and then the phone went dead.
Dash (—)	• To indicate an interruption in a direct quote • To introduce a phrase or clause that summarizes, emphasizes or contrasts what precedes it • To show hesitation • To replace an offensive word • To show a sudden change of mind	Adam shouted, "Watch out for the l—!" Sophie didn't see the lamppost and walked into it. *The Handmaid's Tale, Alias Grace, The Blind Assassin, Oryx and Crake*—these are all famous books by Margaret Atwood. "I think I—er—should go." "Oh s—!" he shouted, as he hit his thumb with the hammer. "Let's go right—no, go left!"
Brackets [ ]	• To clarify or explain information in a direct quote	"She [the mother] called the principal."

EXCEPTIONS

- Abbreviations in the form of acronyms do not normally use periods.
  CBC, NHL, UNO, WWF
- Acronyms that are spoken as a word do not use periods.
  NAFTA, NASA, UNESCO
- Some common abbreviations do not use periods, for example:
  FYI (= for your information)
  RSVP (= Répondez s'il vous plaît)
  asap (= as soon as possible)

Use of quotation marks

1 When commas and quotation marks are used together, commas always go inside quotation marks.

"Just a minute," he shouted.

2 Semicolons and colons always go outside quotation marks.

There is an important point made in the article, "Canadian Schools Today": an educated population is essential for the future of Canada.

I like listening to Rihanna's "Diamonds"; however, I don't understand all the lyrics.

Note that quotation marks are not used in reported speech.

See Reported Speech, page 91.

She said the concert had been postponed.

MORE INFORMATION

A period is called "dot" when we refer to websites and e-mail addresses.

www**.**erpi**.**com = www (**dot**) erpi (**dot**) com

A period is called "point" when we refer to decimal numbers.

0**.**67 = zero **point** six seven

19.2 Capitalization

Canadian Wayne Gretzky played in the **NHL** in **Edmonton** for many years.

When do you use a capital letter?

Use a capital letter for the following: ⟶ ↑ See Nouns, page 9.

Function	Examples
The first word of a sentence	**M**any children swim in the public pool.
First and last names	Alice **M**unro
The pronoun *I*	Tan and **I** watched a movie.
The first word in a direct quote	Mom said, "**D**on't be late for supper."
Each letter in most acronyms	**CBC, NASA, NHL, WWF, UNESCO**
Languages Nationalities, races Religions	I'm learning **E**nglish. She's **C**hinese. **C**atholicism, **H**induism, **I**slam
Towns, cities Countries Geographical features	**G**ranby, **N**ew **Y**ork **C**anada, the **U**nited **S**tates of **A**merica **L**ake **S**uperior, **M**ount **A**ssiniboine
Events	**T**oronto **I**nternational **F**ilm **F**estival, **T**he **O**lympic **G**ames
Days Months Holidays	**M**onday **A**pril **N**ew **Y**ear, **E**aster
Planets Stars Constellations	**M**ars **S**irius the **M**ilky **W**ay
Brand names	**V**olcom, **T**ide, **T**im **H**ortons
Organizations Institutions Businesses	**I**nternational **R**ed **C**ross **C**anadian **M**useum for **H**uman **R**ights, **M**cGill **U**niversity **R**oyal **B**ank of **C**anada
School subjects	Right now, we are studying **G**eography.
Job titles, ranks or official titles	The **G**overnor **G**eneral will speak now.

→

Function	Examples
Main words in a title (first word, last word, nouns, pronouns, adjectives, verbs, adverbs, any conjunction or preposition with five letters or more)	*The **O**ld **M**an and th**e Sea***

MORE INFORMATION

Acronyms can be made up of all capital letters or capital and lower-case letters. Lower-case letters are used especially when an acronym contains letters that are not initials.

Interpol = **Inter**national Criminal **Pol**ice Organization
Nabisco = **Na**tional **Bis**cuit **Co**mpany

BE CAREFUL!

Seasons and directions (unless they are part of a name) do not take a capital letter.

fall   **w**inter   **s**pring   **s**ummer
north   **s**outh   **e**ast   **w**est

But: **S**outh **A**merica

Acronyms that have become words are not capitalized.

laser   radar

Articles and determiners as well as prepositions and conjunctions with fewer than five letters do not take a capital letter in a title.

*The Last **of t**he Mohicans*

Unit 20

Phrasal Verbs and Other Words

I **broke up** with Rick, but I **get along** with his brother.

It was just a **mis**understanding.

Do you **write** with your **right** hand or your left?

20.1 Phrasal Verbs

I think I'm **coming down with** a cold.

What is a phrasal verb?

A phrasal verb is a combination of a verb and one or two prepositions or adverbs that changes the meaning of the verb.

I **called** Alyssa today. (meaning: *call)*
I **called off** my date with Alyssa today. (meaning: *cancel*)

When do you use phrasal verbs?

Phrasal verbs are often less formal than the equivalent one-word verbs, so they are used particularly in the following situations:

1. In spoken English

   I can't **figure out** the meaning of the word. (phrasal verb—informal)
   I cannot **determine** the meaning of the word. (one-word verb—formal)

2. In informal written English

   The students **came up with** a project to help seniors. (phrasal verb—informal)
   The students **produced** a project to help seniors. (one-word verb—formal)

Here is a list of common phrasal verbs.

Phrasal verb	Example	Meaning
break down	Our car **broke down** on the way to Florida.	fail to function
	Lisa **broke down** when she heard about the fire.	get upset
break up	Justin just **broke up** with Cristina.	end a relationship
bring up	Don't **bring up** that topic with Emily.	mention
call back	Her doctor's secretary never **called back**.	return a phone call
call off	My meeting was **called off** today.	cancel
carry on	Don't pay attention to his nonsense and **carry on** with your story.	continue
catch up	Simon will have to hurry if he wants to **catch up** with Mario.	get to the same point as someone else
check in(to) / out (of)	We can't **check into** the hotel until four o'clock.	arrive at a hotel, etc.
	We have to **check out of** the hotel by 10 a.m.	leave a hotel, etc.
cheer up	Only chocolate can **cheer** me **up**!	become happier
come back	The store is closed. We'll **come back** later.	return
come up with	Luc **comes up with** the greatest ideas.	find an idea
cut down	Please **cut down** your essay to make it shorter.	reduce
do up	**Do** your coat **up**. It's cold outside.	fasten or close
drop off	I **dropped off** the books at Karen's house this morning.	to leave something or someone somewhere
end up	I **ended up** choosing karate instead of judo.	finally decide
fall apart	I must repair that table before it **falls apart**.	break into pieces
figure out	She couldn't **figure out** how to assemble the new bookcase.	understand something difficult
fill in	Can you **fill in** this application form, please?	complete with information
get across	I can't **get** my idea **across** to this group!	communicate, explain something
get along	I really **get along** with your friend Olivia.	like each other
get around	Now that my grandmother can't drive, she finds it difficult to **get around**.	go from place to place

Phrasal verb	Example	Meaning
get over	Marie has just **gotten over** pneumonia, but she's still weak.	recover from
get up	I usually **get up** at six in the morning.	rise from bed
	The teacher asked his students to **get up** off the floor.	stand
give in	I finally **gave in** to my mother and had my hair cut.	admit defeat
give up	These science questions are too difficult; I **give up**!	stop trying
go out	Eduardo is **going out** with Danielle.	date, have a relationship
go without	No one can **go without** water for more than five days.	be deprived of
go over	Please **go over** this report and tell me if anything is missing.	review
hang on	**Hang on.** I'll be right back.	wait for a moment
hang out	I like **hanging out** with my best friend Lola.	spend time relaxing
keep up	**Keep up** the good work!	continue
let down	I'll never **let** you **down**; I promise.	disappoint
look after	Lauren **looks after** her brothers while her mother is at work.	take care of
look for	I helped my sister **look for** her passport.	try to find
look forward to	We are **looking forward to** finally meeting you in person.	anticipate with pleasure
look up	What does that word mean? **Look** it **up** in the dictionary.	search
make up	She **made up** an unbelievable story.	invent
put up with	You don't have to **put up with** his bad behaviour.	tolerate
put off	We should **put off** our vacation until Mom feels better.	postpone
run into	Yesterday I **ran into** an old friend.	meet by chance
run out	I **ran out** of reasons why we shouldn't go to the shopping mall.	have none left
set aside	I **set aside** some winter clothes for you.	reserve for later use
set up	The technician will **set up** the new computers tomorrow.	install, organize

Phrasal verb	Example	Meaning
sort out	I need to **sort out** all the pictures in my digital camera.	organize, solve a problem
take off	The plane **takes off** at three o'clock.	begin flight (plane)
turn up	Guess who **turned up** at the concert.	make an appearance
work out	Joseph **works out** three times a week.	exercise

20.2 Prefixes and Suffixes

I don't **re**call if your help**ful co**-worker has an **auto**mobile or a **bi**cycle.

What are prefixes?

Prefixes are letters that are added to the beginning of a word to change its meaning. Here is a list of common prefixes.

Prefix	Meaning	Example
anti-	against	**anti**social
auto-	self	**auto**mobile
bi-	two	**bi**cycle
co-	together, with	**co**-worker
de-	opposite, reduce, remove	**de**construct
dis-	opposite, remove, reverse	**dis**abled
ex-	former	**ex**-wife
fore-	earlier, before	**fore**see
hyper-	extreme, too much	**hyper**active
il-, im-, in-, ir-	not	**il**legal, **im**possible, **in**coherent, **ir**responsible
inter-	between	**inter**act
mal-	bad	**mal**function
mis-	wrongly	**mis**understanding
non-	not	**non**productive
out-	more or better	**out**do
over-	too much	**over**protective

Prefix	Meaning	Example
pre-	before	**pre**mature
re-	again	**re**call
tele-	distant	**tele**communications
un-	not	**un**faithful
	opposite	**un**do
under-	not enough	**under**statement

Use a dictionary to find out whether a word has a hyphen after the prefix.

What are suffixes?

Suffixes are letters that are added to the end of the word to change its meaning. Here is a list of common suffixes.

Suffix	Meaning	Example
-age	collection	bagg**age**
-able, -ible	able to	depend**able**, respons**ible**
-al,-ial	having characteristics of	numeric**al**, part**ial**
-en	made of	wood**en**
-ant, -ent	person or thing doing something	serge**ant**, stud**ent**, disinfect**ant**
-er	comparative	bigg**er**
	doer	teach**er**
-est	superlative	tall**est**
-ful	full of	beauti**ful**
-ic	having characteristics of	metall**ic**
-ion, -tion, -ation, -ition	act, process, state or result	opin**ion**, promo**tion**, prepar**ation**, part**ition**
-ive	does or can do something	attract**ive**, definit**ive**
-less	without	harm**less**
-ly	characteristic of	mother**ly**
	adverbial form of an adjective	ful**ly**
-ment	action or process	govern**ment**
-ness	state of	tender**ness**

Suffix	Meaning	Example
-ous, -eous, -ious	with the qualities of, full of	danger**ous**, advantag**eous**, delic**ious**
-y	characterized by	ic**y**

▽ **BE CAREFUL!**

When the final letter of a prefix is the same letter as the first letter of the base word, keep both letters in the word.

Prefix + base word	Incorrect	Correct
co + operate	~~co~~perate	**coo**perate
im + mature	~~im~~ature	**imm**ature
il + legal	~~il~~egal	**ill**egal
mis + spell	~~mis~~pell	**miss**pell
under + rated	~~under~~ated	**underr**ated

20.3 Homonyms

Are you **too** embarrassed **to** reveal your **two** grammar test results?

Please **close** the door **close** to you.

What are homonyms?

There are two kinds of homonyms: **homophones** and **homographs**.

1 **Homophones** are words that have the same pronunciation but different spellings and meanings.

Here is a list of common homophones.

Homophones	Examples	Meanings
ad	My dad put an **ad** in the local newspaper to sell his car.	(noun) advertisement
add	**Add** chocolate chips to your shopping list.	(verb) put something with something else
ate	We **ate** salmon for supper.	(verb) simple past tense of *eat*
eight	Alessandro is **eight** years old.	(number) 8

Homophones	Examples	Meanings
bear	In Banff, we saw a **bear** in the forest.	(noun) large strong animal with thick fur
bare	I love to walk around with **bare** legs and feet in the summer.	(adjective) without clothes
buy	I will **buy** oranges at the market tomorrow.	(verb) pay money to get something
by	The fruit stall is **by** the entrance.	(preposition) near
bye	See you later, OK? **Bye!**	(interjection) abbreviation of *goodbye*
dear	My **dear** friend Anna lives in Ottawa.	(adjective) important and loved
deer	I saw a **deer** in the forest today.	(noun) large wild animal that can run fast
flour	I bought **flour** to make a cake.	(noun) powder from grain used for making bread and cakes
flower	The **flower** pattern on this wallpaper is pretty.	(noun) coloured or white part of a plant used for producing seeds or fruit
for	My brother sent a card **for** his friend's birthday.	(preposition) where or by whom something is intended to be used
four	Do you have **four** dollars in your pocket?	(number) 4
hear	Hello? Can you **hear** me?	(verb) be aware of sound, using your ears
here	**Here** is my parking space at work.	(adverb) in this place
our	**Our** doctor's appointment is in an **hour**.	(possessive adjective) belonging to us
hour		(noun) sixty minutes
knew	When I was ten years old, I **knew** my times tables by heart.	(verb) simple past tense of *know*
new	Do you like my **new** shoes?	(adjective) recently bought, not old
know	I don't **know** what her name is.	(verb) have information about something
no	**No**, I don't want any dessert.	(adverb) negative reply
right	Turn **right** at the second stop sign.	(adverb) direction, opposite of left
write	Kate loves to **write** stories.	(verb) produce, create, form letters with a pen or pencil

Homophones	Examples	Meanings
their	Mark and Andy are reading **their** books.	(possessive adjective) belonging to them
there	Put your bag over **there** on the desk.	(adverb) in that place
they're	**They're** happy with **their** choice of books.	(personal pronoun and verb) abbreviation of *they are*
to	I'm going **to** the store **to** buy some fudge.	(prep) in the direction of / part of infinitive *to buy*
too	Fudge is **too** sweet for my taste.	(adverb) more than is acceptable
two	Gabriel has **two** brothers and a sister.	(number) 2
wear	**Wear** your warm coat. It's cold outside.	(verb) have on your body
where	**Where** do you want to go on vacation?	(adverb) in/to which place
your	**Your** dog is very friendly.	(possessive adjective) belonging to you
you're	**You're** still doing your homework!	(personal pronoun / verb) contraction of *you are*

2 **Homographs** are words that are spelled the same but have different meanings and may be pronounced differently.

Here are some examples of homographs.

Homograph	Examples	Meanings
bow	At the end of the show, the cast took a **bow**.	(noun) act of bending your body to show thanks or respect
	Robin Hood shot many enemies with his **bow** and arrow.	(noun) weapon made of a long piece of wood and a tight string
	Grace tied the ribbon into a big **bow**.	(noun) a knot made of ribbon, string, shoelaces, etc.
close	My friend lives **close** to me.	(adjective) near
	Please **close** your books.	(verb) shut
content	I am **content** with my results.	(adjective) satisfied
	It's important to check the sugar **content** of drinks.	(noun) amount of a substance contained in something
desert	When we travelled through the **desert**, we took a lot of water with us and stayed in the car.	(noun) place where it is hot, very dry and usually sandy
	If he comes toward us, don't **desert** me!	(verb) abandon

Homograph	Examples	Meanings
lead	This pipe is very heavy. It must be made of **lead**.	(noun) soft, heavy, grey metal
	Follow me. I'll **lead** the way.	(verb) take someone somewhere by going in front
object	A vase is an **object** in which you can put flowers.	(noun) something that can be touched and seen
	"I **object**," said the lawyer.	(verb) oppose something, disagree with someone
present	I was **present** in class today.	(adjective) not absent
	I bought a **present** for your birthday.	(noun) gift
	Let me **present** my new friend David.	(verb) introduce formally
tear	A **tear** ran slowly down her cheek.	(noun) drop of liquid from eye when crying
	Don't **tear** your pants when you bend down!	(verb) rip apart
wind	The **wind** was so strong that it blew the tree down.	(noun) moving air
	The road will **wind** around the mountain on its way to the top.	(verb) turn or twist something around something else

20.4 Synonyms and Antonyms

I like my **new** car better than my **old** one.

What are synonyms and antonyms?

A synonym is a word that has the same meaning as or similar meaning to another word.

An antonym is a word that has the opposite meaning of another word.

When do you use synonyms and antonyms?

Use synonyms and antonyms in writing for these situations:

• To bring words to life
• To make writing more dramatic
• To avoid being repetitive
• To be more specific
• To vary and enrich the vocabulary used in writing

We **like going** to Florida for its **nice** weather. →
We **enjoy travelling** to Florida for its **beautiful** weather.

Here are some examples of synonyms and antonyms.

Common word	Synonyms	Antonyms
bad	corrupt, harmful, loss-making, sinful, unfair, vicious, wrong	beneficial, good, honest, profitable, right, worthy
beautiful	exquisite, handsome, lovely, pretty, stunning	grotesque, hideous, plain, repulsive, ugly
come	advance, approach, attend, visit	depart, go, leave
crazy	delirious, demented, deranged, insane, mad	balanced, reasonable, sane, sensible, smart
go	depart, leave, ride, travel, walk	advance, approach, come, remain, stay
good	able, adequate, attractive, beneficial, ethical, excellent, favourable, pleasant, proper, sensible, well-behaved	bad, disagreeable, evil, horrible, incompetent, naughty, poor, unattractive, wicked
like (verb)	adore, approve of, cherish, enjoy, love	abhor, detest, disapprove of, dislike, hate, loathe
new	fresh, latest, modern, recent	ancient, antique, dated, old, used, vintage, worn
nice	attractive, beautiful, friendly, lovely, pleasant, wonderful	awful, disgusting, horrible, nasty, ugly
see	contemplate, glimpse, notice, observe, spot, watch	be blind, miss, overlook
think	cogitate, consider, contemplate, dream, ponder, reflect	dismiss, disregard, ignore

Use a thesaurus to find synonyms of words.

20.5 Commonly Misused Words

Here is a list of words that are commonly misused.

Misused words	Examples	Meanings
accept	I'm going to **accept** the invitation to the party.	(verb) receive willingly
except	Everyone can go, **except** Erin.	(preposition) with the exclusion of
advice	He took his father's **advice** and spoke to his teacher.	(noun) suggestion or recommendation
advise	I **advise** you to get the best grades you can.	(verb) suggest, give advice

Misused words	Examples	Meanings
affect	This test won't **affect** your final grade.	(verb) do something that produces a change or an effect
effect	The change in the weather could be an **effect** of climate change.	(noun) change, result
choice	You have to make a **choice**: buy the computer or go on vacation.	(noun) the act of choosing
choose	If I were you, I'd **choose** the vacation.	(verb) select freely
chose	Dylan **chose** to buy the computer.	(verb) *choose* in the simple past tense
desert	We travelled through the Sahara **desert**.	(noun) place where it is hot, very dry and usually sandy
dessert	My favourite **dessert** is ice cream.	(noun) sweet food served after the main part of a meal
eligible	Employees of the company are not **eligible** to take part in the competition.	(adjective) qualified to participate
legible	Her handwriting is not very good, but it's **legible**.	(adjective) capable of being read
illegible	My doctor's handwriting is completely **illegible**.	(adjective) not legible
envelop	A thick fog started to **envelop** the houses.	(verb) enclose
envelope	Send the form to the address on the **envelope**.	(noun) flat paper container
know	I don't **know** where Ryan lived before.	(verb) be aware of a fact or truth
now	**Now** he lives in Ontario.	(adverb) at the present time
loose	Your earring is **loose**.	(adjective) not securely attached
lose	Be careful you don't **lose** it.	(verb) fail to keep
of	Most **of** my friends are going on the trip.	(preposition) belonging to
off	The plane took **off** at midnight.	(adverb) away, not on
than	Nicole is much taller **than** her sister.	(conjunction) used to compare or contrast things
then	We ordered a pizza, and **then** we watched the movie.	(adverb) at a particular time in the past or future

Note that many words have more than one meaning. Use a dictionary to find the different meanings of a word.

Irregular Verbs Chart

Base form	Simple past	Past participle
arise	arose	arisen
awake	awoke	awoken
be	was / were	been
bear	bore	borne
beat	beat	beaten
become	became	become
begin	began	begun
bend	bent	bent
bet	bet	bet
bid	bid	bid
bind	bound	bound
bite	bit	bitten
bleed	bled	bled
blow	blew	blown
break	broke	broken
breed	bred	bred
bring	brought	brought
broadcast	broadcast / broadcasted	broadcast / broadcasted
build	built	built
burn	burned / burnt	burned / burnt
burst	burst	burst
buy	bought	bought
cast	cast	cast
catch	caught	caught
choose	chose	chosen
cling	clung	clung
come	came	come

Base form	Simple past	Past participle
cost	cost	cost
creep	crept	crept
cut	cut	cut
deal	dealt	dealt
dig	dug	dug
dive	dived / dove	dived
do	did	done
draw	drew	drawn
dream	dreamed / dreamt	dreamed / dreamt
drink	drank	drunk
drive	drove	driven
eat	ate	eaten
fall	fell	fallen
feed	fed	fed
feel	felt	felt
fight	fought	fought
find	found	found
fit	fit / fitted	fit / fitted
flee	fled	fled
fling	flung	flung
fly	flew	flown
forbid	forbade	forbidden
forecast	forecast / forecasted	forecast / forecasted
forget	forgot	forgotten
forgive	forgave	forgiven
freeze	froze	frozen
get	got	gotten / got
give	gave	given
go	went	gone

Base form	Simple past	Past participle
grind	ground	ground
grow	grew	grown
hang	hung	hung
have	had	had
hear	heard	heard
hide	hid	hidden
hit	hit	hit
hold	held	held
hurt	hurt	hurt
keep	kept	kept
kneel	kneeled / knelt	kneeled / knelt
know	knew	known
lay	laid	laid
lead	led	led
lean	leaned / leant	leaned / leant
leap	leaped / leapt	leaped / leapt
learn	learned / learnt	learned / learnt
leave	left	left
lend	lent	lent
let	let	let
lie	lay	lain
light	lit / lighted	lit / lighted
lose	lost	lost
make	made	made
mean	meant	meant
meet	met	met
pay	paid	paid
put	put	put
quit	quit	quit

Base form	Simple past	Past participle
read	read	read
rid	rid	rid
ride	rode	ridden
ring	rang	rung
rise	rose	risen
run	ran	run
say	said	said
see	saw	seen
seek	sought	sought
sell	sold	sold
send	sent	sent
set	set	set
shake	shook	shaken
shed	shed	shed
shine	shone / shined	shone / shined
shoot	shot	shot
show	showed	shown / showed
shrink	shrank / shrunk	shrunk
shut	shut	shut
sing	sang	sung
sink	sank	sunk
sit	sat	sat
sleep	slept	slept
slide	slid	slid
slit	slit	slit
smell	smelled / smelt	smelled / smelt
sneak	sneaked / snuck	sneaked / snuck
speak	spoke	spoken
speed	sped / speeded	sped / speeded

Base form	Simple past	Past participle
spell	spelled / spelt	spelled / spelt
spend	spent	spent
spill	spilled / spilt	spilled / spilt
spin	spun	spun
spit	spat / spit	spat / spit
split	split	split
spoil	spoiled / spoilt	spoiled / spoilt
spread	spread	spread
spring	sprang	sprung
stand	stood	stood
steal	stole	stolen
stick	stuck	stuck
sting	stung	stung
stink	stank / stunk	stunk
strike	struck	struck / stricken
string	strung	strung
strive	strove / strived	striven / strived
swear	swore	sworn
sweep	swept	swept
swell	swelled	swelled / swollen
swim	swam	swum
swing	swung	swung
take	took	taken
teach	taught	taught
tear	tore	torn
tell	told	told
think	thought	thought
throw	threw	thrown
thrust	thrust	thrust

Base form	Simple past	Past participle
understand	understood	understood
upset	upset	upset
wake	woke	woken
wear	wore	worn
weep	wept	wept
win	won	won
wind	wound	wound
withdraw	withdrew	withdrawn
write	wrote	written

MORE INFORMATION

Some verbs have more than one form in the simple past and past participle. In this case, the first form shown is more commonly used in North America.

Index